35.—

Philosophy at the
Limit

PROBLEMS OF MODERN EUROPEAN THOUGHT

Series editors
Alan Montefiore
Jonathan Rée
Jean-Jacques Lecercle

Philosophy at the Limit

DAVID WOOD

London
UNWIN HYMAN
Boston   Sydney   Wellington

© David Wood 1990

This book is copyright under the Berne Convention. No
reproduction without permission. All rights reserved.

Published by the Academic Division of
Unwin Hyman Ltd
15/17 Broadwick Street, London W1V 1FP, UK

Unwin Hyman Inc.,
955 Massachusetts Avenue, Cambridge, Mass., 02139, USA

Allen & Unwin (Australia) Ltd,
8 Napier Street, North Sydney, NSW 2060, Australia

Allen & Unwin (New Zealand) Ltd in association with the
Port Nicholson Press Ltd,
Compusales Building, 75 Ghuznee Street, Wellington 1, New Zealand

First published in 1990

British Library Cataloguing in Publication Data

Wood, David, *1946*–
    Philosophy at the limit.
    1. European Philosophy
    I. Title
    190

ISBN 0–04–445625–5
ISBN 0–04–445624–7 pbk

Library of Congress Cataloging in Publication Data

Available from the Library of Congress

Typeset in 10/12 point Garamond
Printed in Great Britain by
Billing and Sons Ltd, Worcester

26.5.93

Contents

Editors' foreword

During most of the twentieth century, philosophers in the English-speaking world have had only partial and fleeting glimpses of the work of their counterparts in continental Europe. In the main, English-language philosophy has been dominated by the exacting ideals of conceptual analysis and even of formal logic, while 'continental philosophy' has ventured into extensive substantive discussions of literary, historical, psycho-analytic and political themes. With relatively few exceptions, the relations between the two traditions have been largely uncomprehending and hostile.

In recent years, however, continental witers such as Heidegger, Adorno, Sartre, de Beauvoir, Habermas, Foucault, Althusser, Lacan and Derrida have been widely read in English translation, setting the terms of theoretical debate in such fields as literature, social theory, cultural studies, Marxism and feminism. The suspicions of the analytical philosophers have not, however, been pacified; and the import of such continental philosophy has mostly been isolated from original philosophical work in English.

The PROBLEMS OF MODERN EUROPEAN THOUGHT series is intended to help break down this isolation. The books in the series will be original philosophical essays in their own right, from authors familiar with the procedures of analytical philosophy. Each book will present a well-defined range of themes from continental philosophy, and will presuppose little, if any formal, philosophical training of its readers.

Alan Montefiore
Jonathan Rée
Jean-Jacques Lecercle

Acknowledgements

I would like to thank the editors of the series – Alan Montefiore, Jonathan Rée and Jean-Jacques Lecercle – for their patience, encouragement and constructive suggestions. This book has benefited considerably from their critical attentions. Among the friends and colleagues who, often inadvertently, have influenced the arguments in this book I would particularly mention Christine Battersby, Andrew Benjamin, Robert Bernasconi, Jay Bernstein, Paul Davies, David Krell, John Llewelyn, Christopher Norris, John Sallis, Charles Scott and Martin Warner. Special thanks are due to Jacques Derrida whose lectures at Balliol over twenty years ago and subsequent writing have been both an inspiration and a challenge. I also owe a great deal to the many participants in our series of Warwick Workshops in Continental Philosophy, and our Centre for Research in Philosophy and Literature conferences in the last few years. These chapters were tried out on unsuspecting audiences at Middlesex Polytechnic, the Open University, the Universities of Leeds, Essex, Oxford, Northwestern, McMaster, Loyola (Chicago), and York (Toronto), as well as meetings of the International Association for Philosophy and Literature, at the kind invitation of Hugh Silverman whose friendship has meant a great deal. I would also like to thank Claire L'Enfant, Jane Harris-Matthews and Lauren Osborne for being, at various stages of the process, everything that editors should be. Finally I apologize to Mary, Michael and Christopher who must sometimes think they have thrown in their lot with a creature from another planet.

Introduction

It is clear, then, that the word 'limit' has as many senses as 'beginning'; more ... in fact, for every beginning is a limit but not every limit is a beginning.

(Aristotle, *Metaphysics*)

The concept of a noumenon is ... a merely limiting concept, the function of which is to curb the pretensions of sensibility.

(Kant, *Critique of Pure Reason*)

A thing is what it is, only in and by reason of its limit ... Man, if he wishes to be actual, must be-there-and-then, and to this end he must set a limit to himself.

(Hegel, *Logic*)

Man has the impulse to run up against the limits of language ... This running up against Kierkegaard also recognised ... (as running up against Paradox). This running-up against the limits of language is ethics.

(Wittgenstein, 'On Heidegger on Being and Dread')

The limits of my language are the limits of my world.

(Wittgenstein, *Tractatus Logico-Philosophicus*)

To write otherwise. To delimit the space of a closure no longer analogous to what philosophy can represent for itself under this name, according to a straight or circular line enclosing a homogeneous space.

(Derrida, *Margins*)

Philosophy is an everlasting fire, sometimes damped down by setting itself limits, then flaring into new life as it consumes them. Every field of inquiry is limited, but philosophy has an essential relation to the question of limits, to its own limits. When it is not claiming to be able to determine the boundaries of science, or the individual sciences, it none the less understands itself by contrast to such disciplines. Aristotle, famously, defines metaphysics not as a science of this or that kind of being, but of being *qua* being. And the fact that philosophy typically has defined itself in contrast to other disciplines has been a source of the perennial attraction of philosophy, for it promises insights of a quite different order. There was a time when the alternative to the sensuous order was assumed to be the supersensuous, and philosophy had to compete with religion for access to a realm beyond this world. Philosophy derived its privilege from the infinite, leaving the finite world to opinion, or to science. Kant changed all that, not simply by curbing the pretensions of a philosophy that knew no limits to its scope, but by redefining the kind of thinking and the kind of knowledge that philosophy could call its own. Philosophy need not soar above and beyond the limits set by other fields of inquiry; it found its true role in establishing the boundaries and conditions of such disciplines, a function they themselves were unable to perform. Philosophy came to specialize in conceptual and theoretical clarification, and to this day the Kantian influence has persisted in this approach. But our capacity to describe it as an 'approach' in this way already marks the move beyond it.

The recognition of historical transformations both in the frameworks of sciences and in the philosophies that have had to think them, exposes philosophy either to an attempt to subject conceptual change to a further conceptual order (classically Hegel's Reason), or to abandon conceptual change to empiricism. The implausibility of the former is matched only by the unsatisfactoriness of the latter. Philosophy finds itself confronting a limit to the scope of its own carefully considered activity. The recognition that philosophical thinking is not conducted in some pure logical space, but in more or less messy languages, poses another key difficulty to philosophy. If it chooses to translate its problems into a mere formal language, any success it might have runs the risk of being judged a merely formal solution. (Contagious diseases could be eliminated if people lived in sealed containers.) If on the other hand it understands its natural linguistic form as unavoidable, there are still a multitude of strategies, stylistic or textual options allowing one to make the best of this condition. There is, however, a powerful thesis to the effect that the concepts with which (e.g. post-pre-Socratic) philosophers have been engaged, are entangled in an invisible and distorting web often called metaphysics. Perhaps *conceptuality itself* is threatened. The response to this raises the question of strategy to new levels of urgency. Experience too constitutes a limit to faith in the conceptual, whether these are fundamental pre-conceptual intuitions (for example, Fichte's sense of self-activity) or limit-experiences (such as Kierkegaard's *Angst*, or Sartre's *Nausea*).[1]

For a philosophy that conceives of itself as an essentially conceptual activity, each of these dimensions in its own way interrupts that self-containment with an excess, and confronts it with limits.

The book is devoted to the results of confronting some of these limits. Perhaps 'negotiating' would be better than 'confronting'. For one of the central issues is whether overcoming such limits is not itself an illusion, a burden – a limitation. Is not the dream of totalization only a peculiarly *unreflective* way of 'taking account of' limits? It would, for example, be a tragic misdirection of one's energies to approach the problem of communication by attempting an absolute anticipation or advance calculation of the response of the other. The recognition of otherness is the recognition that recognition is *essentially* limited, an openness that does not enclose. Such a limitation is not one that challenges us to overcome it. *Overcoming the temptation to such a response* is overcoming a limitation! Here what is limited turns out not to be our knowledge or grasp of the object, or our conceptual clarity, but our assumptions about the ideal that 'grasping' represents. Such a result illustrates quite well the claim that philosophy has an essential relation to the question of limits, and its own limits.

The structure of the thought that would see a limit in the desire to overcome all limits is both complex and exemplary. Limits are always limits to some project or desire or ambition. But such projects are themselves open to scrutiny. And if they are tied in to certain very general understandings of philosophy, then enormous consequences may follow that scrutiny. What Sartre said about a fallen log in one's path is true of limits in general, that they are *for us*, relative to a particular philosophical project. In coming across a limit, we come across a reflection of ourselves.

Here the strategies of deconstruction are most instructive. For it was Derrida's early claim that the history of philosophy was bound up with a very general desire, or valuation – the drive to presence. Any limit encountered in the course of such a pursuit would have to be overcome. The outcome would eventually be an unmediated relation to the ground of truth, in the shape of pure intuition, the absolute, self-understanding, the other person and so on. But there is an essential naivety in thinking of limits simply as 'to be overcome' if the moment of confrontation can still be a moment of reflective insight.[2]

Not everyone has found references to the metaphysics of presence illuminating. And certainly the value of conjoining so many otherwise diverse philosophical ambitions must be weighed against the dangers of apparent assimilation. But the inescapable fertility of Derrida's general claim lies in the way it probes what we could call the topology of thinking. It both allows and forces us to rethink the question of ends, of beginnings, of margins, of limits, thresholds – the very space of philosophy. There is no thinking of *limits* that does not deploy a certain model of space.

Typically, however, our thinking is hopelessly bound to a model drawn from visual representations in which a two-dimensional homogeneous space is separated by a line from other such spaces. These spaces may be determined in a certain way, or as yet undetermined ('the Unknown begins here'). But the structure of the limit commonly deployed is that of the simple and continuous dividing line on a two-dimensional surface.

It is not difficult to see why. Logic seems to tell us that things have to be on one side of a line or another. Imagination supports this view. Even on a curved surface we naturally draw areas, regions, that exclude other areas and include whatever lies inside them. Our assured and intuitive basis for deploying the inside/outside distinction is confirmed by every squirrel who cracks open a nut, and every child who unwraps a birthday present.

There is no doubt that philosophical thinking is often unconsciously, and often quite openly determined, by such topological intuitions. Indeed, if the connection between geometry and intuition is as close as reading Plato might lead us to believe, we might come to think that the very source of intuition lay not in anything primitive or natural, but precisely in what we could call logically schematized representation.[3] Much of what we think of as clarity and distinctness rests on topological hygiene, on good housekeeping: tidying spaces, mending fences, defining boundaries. If it were the business of philosophy to act as an under-labourer,[4] and perhaps site manager, for the constructions of the sciences, it might be that the guidance provided by such underlying schemata would prove invaluable. But such a subservient role could not survive the revaluation of the status of the sciences that Kant and Hegel set in motion. Kant showed that the very possibility of the sciences, and their objects, rested on transcendental conditions whose articulation was not itself a science or an object. For Kant, space (and of course time) were forms of intuition, which on the one hand might suggest a subjective contribution to the various kinds of limits we take ourselves merely to come across, and on the other would provide a *grounding* (for example, in the shape of a *deduction*) for the schema involved, which would not be subjective in any privative sense, but in a transcendental sense. Since Kant's day the hegemony of Euclid and Newton has faded, and we are much more inclined to understand the transcendental more relativistically, either in terms of mathematical or physical models, or distinctive modes of experience, or language. Whichever route one takes, what seems to open up are much more complex topological possibilities which radically unsettle any simple assignation of inside and outside, and hence of limits. In each case what is exploded is the privilege of a certain simple and exclusive mode of representation, often associated with vision, but which already gives vision a specific ordering. From mathematics and physics, we have Klein bottles (in which the outside seems to be enclosed within), black holes (at the edge of which – the 'event horizon' – space and time are both transformed, putting the idea of the edge into question), and numerous other less famous challenges to our representational habits. Experience is no less fertile an area, particularly when embodiment is given a proper role. Every orifice of the body is the site of boundary ambiguity, and powerful operations of boundary maintenance. Books could be written on the mouth alone. But in the interplay between the body as lived in various ways and the body as representing and as represented to itself there is scope for considerable stratified and interweaving complexity. Consider the child in warm pyjamas who draws the curtains and is delighted with the sight of falling snow. And who thinks of giving the snowman a coat with buttons to keep him warm. At one level, the distinction between inside and outside is very clear, and is marked by the window. And yet the child's delight at the events outside rests on the barrier being breached, on the possibility of going outside to play. And the concern for the snowman involves an extension of conditions of inner contentment (warmth) to an inappropriate outer. The relation between inner and outer first thought of as subject and object of experience is subverted by imagination, by desire, by memory, and by time. It is subverted quite generally by intentionality. For Descartes the distinction between mind and body was evidenced by the shift from transparency to opacity. We are much more likely to see the line between the two as problematic. Mirrors – and looking glasses – are notorious for the boundary complexity they generate. We need not, with Foucault, dwell on the multiple planes of Velasquez's *Las Meninas*.[5] An adequate description of the everyday experience of looking at oneself in a mirror is challenge enough. Merleau-Ponty describes the position of the body in the world as one of ambiguity, and later uses the term *chiasm* ('every relation with being is *simultaneously* a taking and a being taken') to capture the duality of our being in the world.[6] Once experience is no longer thought of either as a passive reception of a given field or as an active invention, the shape of which is prescribed by subjective laws, no determinate account of its limits will suffice, whether of a single experience, or of experience in general. Merleau-Ponty was increasingly impressed by the impact of language on experience, and on our thinking about experience, and it is language that makes the third distinctive contribution to subverting the Euclidean topology of limits. If language is thought of as an instrument wielded by a knowing subject with an essentially transparent and manipulable cognitive content ('words mean what I want them to mean'), and if it is subordinated to traditional epistemological goals, then the kind of subversion I have indicated does not arise. However once language is seen to have its own thickness, density, body, its own rules and unruliness; once it is seen to pervade our being, any attempt at such a subordination is crippled. A traditional analytical approach might say that words like inside and outside, internal and external, limit, boundary, beyond, transcendent, other, are inherently ambiguous and need specifying, defining. It is of course quite true that these terms are ambiguous and under-specified, and that we always need to know something more specific about how they are being used. Matters are more complex however. Where are we standing when we take up this dis-stance? Are we outside language, peering in? Or inside part of it, reflecting on another distinct part? Are subjects deploying language, or is our very subjectivity constituted by language? Can we even employ these oppositions at all helpfully here?

If there is one thing Nietzsche, Wittgenstein, Heidegger, Foucault and Derrida have each taught us it is that the traditional epistemologically centred demarcation of the subject's relation to the world, in which knowledge (especially perceptual) provides the guiding thread, is fatally undercut by the linguistic character of our being. And *language* understood in this way cannot be assigned a place within the traditional topological scheme of regions and linear limits. It is not merely a thickening of the boundary, or the darkening of a mediating lens. It is the irreversible displacement of all insight drawn from the visual field, even when this is reflected through an active subject. Those who, in the name of enlightenment, would have us flee the necessary entanglement which this state prescribes for us are the false prophets of imaginary dawns.

Notes

1 The confrontation of philosophy with limits is inseparable from that of the philosopher. Our finite and mortal existence is no mere external damper on an otherwise everlasting activity; it conditions us in our very being, as Hegel and Heidegger well knew. Mortality is a limit that makes certain kinds of essential human determinations possible, and, indeed, for Heidegger, opens up the whole dimension of *possibility*. To think of one's own death is not merely to contemplate a certain topic of thought, but ultimately to put in question the very activity (if that it is) of thinking, the being of the thinker, and of the other. Experience too poses challenges to philosophy by which it comes to grasp itself in a more sanguine way. For we have experiences that seem to outrun the categories and broader conceptual apparatus we have for dealing with them. Kierkegaard and Heidegger speak of *Angst*, Sartre speaks of *Nausea*, Jaspers of limit-experiences, Nietzsche of the experience of eternal recurrence, and Levinas writes of the explosion of the intentional relation brought about by the Other.

2 Such thinking can be found in Heidegger's remarks: 'Yet a regard for metaphysics still prevails even in the intention to overcome metaphysics. Therefore, our task is to cease all overcoming, and leave metaphysics to itself' (*On Time and Being* [1962], trans. J. Stambaugh (New York: Harper & Row, 1972), p. 25).

3 Derrida's introduction to Husserl's *The Origin of Geometry* [1962], trans. J. Leavey (Brighton: Harvester, 1978) is extraordinarily valuable here.

4 I have in mind Locke's description of philosophy in *An Essay Concerning Human Understanding* (London: Dent, [1690] 1961).

5 See his frontispiece to *The Order of Things* (London: Tavistock, 1970). Painting would provide another extraordinarily rich vein to mine in considering the subversion of the limit. Foucault's *This Is not a Pipe* (Berkeley and Los Angeles: University of California Press, 1983) is a classic example.

6 See his *Phenomenology of Perception* [1945] (London: Routledge, 1962), and, later, *The Visible and the Invisible* [1964] (Evanston: Northwestern, 1968).

Philosophy at the Limit

1

The faces of silence

I

It is hard not to be impressed by the way in which radio interviewees manage to reply so promptly to the most difficult of questions. We are of course witnessing an illusion for which a good editor can take the credit. Dr Murke worked as an interviewer and editor for a radio station and spent much of his waking life clipping out long pauses from recorded interviews. But he did not just throw away the clippings. He spliced together all the gaps, the pauses, the hesitations, the moments of dumbstruck speechlessness that would have spoilt the even flow of a radio broadcast, into a single tape – his collection of silences – to which he would listen over and over again in the long evenings. This is the gist of a short story by Heinrich Boll 'Dr Murke's Collection of Silences'. What sustains the story is the possibility of distinguishing between different silences in terms of their different significances.

At the most extreme, and at this everyday empirical level, there is an obvious difference between the silence of someone who has not heard that he is being asked a question, the silence of someone who does not know what to say, and the silence of someone who refuses to answer. A classification of the various possibilities would be a fascinating chapter in a theory of speech acts. But my interest in silence is different. I want to ask whether there can be a necessary silence, something that cannot be said. I begin with a dark suspicion – that our whole way of thinking about limits and whether or not they can be overcome is mistakenly visual. Might it not be a fundamental mistake to think of such limits as any sort of a wall or barrier in some sort of space?

The need for silence could be said to face us at the limits of language. But what is meant by 'limit' here ? The most obvious meaning of 'limit' is that of a boundary which marks off whatever is on one side from whatever is on the other. But there are immediate problems in coming

1

to understand such a limit. When Lucretius argued against the finitude of the world he exposed the problem nicely. If, when I come to the edge of the world, I throw my javelin, it will either stop, in which case there is something stopping it, or it will continue, in which case it continues into something. Either way, if there is something beyond – be it a barrier or a space – it cannot be the edge of the universe. An analogous problem faces us. How can we describe the limits of language without describing what lies each side of the limit and thus contradicting the claim that it is the limit?[1]

Much of the difficulty arises from the attempt to visualize such limits using notions, pictures or schemes drawn from geography, geometry or real estate. These models offer us something like a continuous space, divided internally. If we draw a circle on a page there is an obvious sense in which the circumference constitutes the limit of the circle. It is in such a way that signs announce 'City Limits'. In these cases something of the same order continues outside the limits – whether it is just space, or, more fully, roads, trees, animal life, air, etc. But in the case of language, if there are limits to its application it is hard to see what could continue the same, or at what level there can be a continuity to sustain a limit. 'Being able to be talked about' does not seem to be a property in any ordinary sense. Indeed as soon as we try to imagine what it would be like for something not to have this 'property' in some strong sense of 'not to have' we find our imagination grinding to a halt, as if we were trying to imagine a square without corners.

And yet if the idea of a limit to language is to play any role in our thinking we must be able to say something about this limit even if it does not commit us to saying anything, or anything direct, about what lies outside it. My central claim in this chapter will seem paradoxical: that there is a strong and important sense in which the idea of there being something that cannot be said is itself an *effect* of language. To give focus to the discussion I shall begin by looking at one of the most plausible candidates for a region or domain that cannot be described: experience, or certain sorts of experience.

It might be said, and indeed several phenomenologists have, that while some experiences can be described, they can never be fully described, and, whether or not they can, they can never be captured in language. Let us start with a strong claim – that some experiences cannot be described: suppose we read in some tale of mystery and imagination that the hero, incautiously visiting a notoriously desolate spot one night, experienced an 'unnameable horror'. Further elaboration seems called for. But perhaps the novelist does not tell us any more except to say that the man was deranged by the experience. Surely there is a fairly simple account to be given here – perhaps a very illuminating one – that the experience was not one of (a) horror which happened to be unnameable/indescribable – but that the experience was in whole or in part constituted by it not being able to be described. (Just as the experience of being surprised by some event is constituted by one's not having expected it to happen.) The experience is not simply an experience of some object or event, but the living through of a very particular reaction to some object or event etc. I may indeed be able, negatively, to describe my reaction to it, but it seems to have a quality, and certainly a force, that such descriptions do not seem to deal with. To take an example from a philosopher (if not from philosophy) consider Roquentin's description of a root in Sartre's *Nausea*, or rather, his description – which trails off as language begins to fail him – of his experience of the root:

> Knotty, inert, nameless, it fascinated me, filled my eyes, repeatedly brought me back to its own existence. It was no use my repeating: 'It is a root'– that didn't work any more . . . when I took my foot away, I saw that the bark was still black. Black? I felt the word subside, empty itself of its meaning with an extraordinary speed. (p. 186)

It is significant, of course, that this experience is a reflective experience in the sense that the experiencer is thinking through the difficulty of using language at the very moment he is having the experience. And, as with horror, an essential aspect of the experience is this failure of language. That failure is not an added extra. If horror and here nausea are typical responses to coming up against the limits of language, we might think it an urgent matter to understand the nature of such limits. If I might venture a temporary diagnosis: in the case of horror, the experience is that of the breakdown of the protective role played by our fundamental interpretive frameworks. Somehow we become aware of something which seems to pose a threat, while recognizing that we do not know how to conceptualize it. Alternatively, we may know exactly what it is but realize that *knowing* it does not help at all. We shall return to this.

The second sense in which experience can offer limits to language can be seen in any experience whatsoever – that there is no such thing as a complete description. Think of any reasonably complex experience – that of a landscape, for example. You could describe it at great length, and just when you thought there was nothing left to say, another angle may strike you. It could be argued that such descriptive incompleteness is not at all based on the intrinsic richness of some original experience of the landscape, but on the unlimited possibilities of further reflection on the landscape (and on the experience of the landscape). This is surely what is going on when I see a new angle from which to describe it . . . But far from undermining the indescribability thesis, this can be used to strengthen it. For reflection surely appears at the very moment at which one begins to describe the experience, to 'put it into words'. Suppose you realize while driving along that you have just missed a pedestrian by inches. You think back. Did you in fact see the person about to cross the road and assume that he (or she) would wait? Did you think that whether or not they had stepped off the kerb there would still be plenty of space to get through? Was the experience ever so resolved as any of these options would ever suggest? And how many stripes were there on the pedestrian crossing? You don't remember. But surely they were there in front of you? They were not hidden in any way. If one can grasp a definite plurality of stripes without noticing how many there were, does not that show that experience operates with a level of inexplicitness that language cannot tolerate, and that reflection always tries to rectify? Not necessarily. One can describe the experience in such a way as to preserve the inexplicitness in which as many questions are asked as answers given, doubts expressed, indeterminacies unresolved. In such descriptions the absence of any explicit decision-making process is indicated. And we could use the word 'some' or 'a number' to indicate an indeterminate awareness of a determinate number of stripes in the crossing. Surely language is quite up to the task if all it has to do is to stay as vague as the original experience? But is this true? Is it not possible that description still transforms experience in a distorting way? If I say 'I crossed the zebra crossing' I do not say whether or not I counted the stripes. This remains true if I say 'It was made up of some black and white stripes'. If I say 'the person was hovering at the side of the street' I do not let on whether the person was obviously male or female, fat or thin, tall or short, had two legs or three, etc. And yet one supposes that 'in the experience itself', prior to our reflection on it, (which may indeed complicate matters), each of these questions will have a particular answer (even if it is sometimes 'Don't know'). Surely the fact that one cannot give that

4

assurance in respect of any finite description constitutes a limit to language?

This takes us close to the third sense of such limits, when applied to experience – the thought that language cannot capture experience. This is a commonplace observation. We might say it of visiting a foreign city, of meeting an impressive person, of listening to music. Here, even if one could give an exhaustive description of the experience, there would still be a difference between the experience and the description that could not be overcome. Imagine trying to tell someone what it felt like to be a soldier in battle. Somehow words will seem hollow compared to the sense of mortal danger . . . One might indeed fall silent.

How ought we to assess the general suggestion that experience constitutes a limit to language? I would pick out three different features that language, or the use of language, is said to possess, by virtue of which these limitations become apparent: generality, explicitness and 'emptiness'.

Consider *generality* first. Roquentin's description of his sense of nausea at the root in the park comes from his somehow feeling that the sheer particularity of the root, its thisness, its being this root and no other . . . was not captured by any description, which could after all apply to any other similar root. Roquentin's nausea results from his recognition that the sheer presence of this root cannot be captured by general concepts or universals. Even when we say 'thisness' we say something that is true of every root, and so divert a confrontation with the particular actual root. Language, in short, recognizes only instances, not individuals.

Second, we could consider *explicitness*. Language steps in where the angels of experience fear to tread. A description has no reserve of answers to questions. It has to make decisions where experience made none.

Finally, there is 'hollowness'/'emptiness' – language just is not the same as an experience. Experiences are real, primary while language is just derivative, secondary.

There is a general reply to all three claims, which would, in effect, treat all these features in a positive rather than a negative way. It was begun by Hegel, and can be found wherever a philosopher feels that experience and language cannot be so easily separated. I will offer two versions here.

But perhaps I could begin with an obvious reply to the third claim – that in effect one of the limits of language in relation to experience is that it can never truly capture it. Sometimes this is just false, as we shall see shortly. But equally it could be thought trivial. Surely it would only be a limitation if it was an intelligible goal for language to *capture experience*,[2] and it is not. It is true that language is not the same thing as experience, and that language can have dealings with experience, but it is not language which is hollow or empty, but the meaning of 'capturing'. Its not being the same as the experiences it describes is a disappointment only to those who imagine for it a fantastic ideal.

Though it may seem perverse, I also want to argue that the claim that language cannot capture experience is false (as well as being a guilty verdict on an empty charge). And this argument bears directly on the question of the generality and the explicitness of language with respect to experience. In answer to the claim that language is explicit and general where experience can be individual and particular and full of complex unresolved nuances, it could be argued that all these are negative features, which language helps to eliminate. Description helps experiences to realize themselves fully, to be fully themselves. An experience (and the act or process of experiencing) is not just some random collection of sensory inputs, but something with a shape and a meaning to it, which may be more or less well developed. And description can serve to bring out this shape and meaning, and so help the experience to come into its own. Some examples: it used to be said that Eastern bloc athletes were trained to verbalize their movements as far as possible, with the aim of perfecting these movements by increasing the level of control and attention. So the high-jumper whose trailing leg keeps knocking over the bar will have to ask himself at the right time where his leg is, to be able to describe his jumping accurately, to *articulate* his action, as we might say. Articulation requires attention and this makes correction possible. Here deficiencies in a complex action are defined in relation to the end towards which it is directed, and language in the form of verbalization helps to eliminate such deficiencies. Or again, take the case of the soldier returning from war. On our previous account he finds no words adequate to convey his experience of being under fire. But perhaps it is also true that he cannot make any sense of his experience as a whole until he reads a newspaper feature which gives his own actions and those of his friends a historical significance, bringing out the latent meaning of his previously vague and disconnected experiences. Such a scenario is not implausible. Here, surely, language is actually coming to the aid of experience,

6

helping it to have the shape and significance one seeks in it. One final example: until I wrote this book, my thinking about silence and the limits of language was fragmented and undeveloped. Now, the whole way I think about it is affected by writing about it. Every student who writes an essay has the same experience. The experience of reading a book is enormously changed by having to write a review of it. In all these cases, language intensifies experience precisely by forcing certain ambiguities to resolve themselves, by inducing reflection, and by raising the particular to the level of the concept, as Hegel would say. Even the lyrical poet knows that language is the friend of experience. When experience preserves itself against language, it merely festers away in the pale recesses of subjectivity. Everything of value in experience can be improved by the objectifying reflection wrought by language.

I am of course resorting here to rhetoric and bare assertion. I am trying to fill out the general claim that language finds no significant limit in 'experience', by showing the contribution language makes to the enhancement of experience. I return to this position shortly, but first I consider another position, which is that experience and language cannot be separated in the way necessary for experience to constitute a limit to language. Experience, on this view, is not a silent movie but a great Babel of voices, or at any rate, however silent it may seem, interwoven with concepts and perceptual schemata, with much of its internal structure derived from language. Rather than deny this – I don't know that I would want to, or how I would set about it – I will simply offer an example, that of dreaming, in which this interweaving of language with experience (especially visual images) is undeniable, and yet in which the consequences for the denial of the limits of language thesis are far from clear-cut.

According to Sigmund Freud, our dreams contain a large quantity of linguistic material in the form of puns, rebuses and other plays on words and with letters. And the two key mechanisms of what he called the dream-work – condensation and displacement – have been linked with those most common of linguistic tropes, metonymy and metaphor. Are dreams not paradigms of the part played by language in experience? (I have no time for the suggestion that dreams are nothing but the imaginary objects of dream-reports, breakfast-time fantasies.) But if dreams are such paradigms, is it not unfortunate that accurate accounts of dreams can be so entirely nonsensical? What passes for an intelligible sequence at the time may involve logical contradictions, confusions of identity and temporal dislocation when carefully described. In what sense can language get to grips with dreams when the structure of dreams is so bizarre and ungrammatical? Even if dreams do involve an interweaving of linguistic material, this does not mean that linguistic descriptions can penetrate its thickets. But if the interweaving of language with experience that we find here in dreams does not in itself open up experience to language, because what is interwoven might only be a certain limited level of language (who would suggest that experience takes the form of sentences?), we have not of course shown that it *does* constitute a limit to language. People are not silent about their dreams. Nor are psychoanalysts, who have developed special forms of explanation and description for dreams. This might suggest a new generalization: that experience, if dreams are anything to go by, is not ready-made for linguistic handling, but requires special care. And we might wonder whether this is not a principle that could be extended to all cases of the apparent limits of language. Silence would be replaced by subtlety and sensitivity.

But the case of horror which we discussed first of all presents us with a difficulty that cannot be skirted so easily, and this difficulty has an extremely interesting form, as we shall see in other cases. If our account is correct, there is, or seems to be, a logical objection to language dealing with horror – or at least that 'unspeakable', 'unutterable' or 'indescribable' horror. For if the experience of horror is, at least in part, the experience of the inadequacy of words, surely there is an *a priori* objection to any attempt to put the experience into words, one with which subtlety and sensitiveness will not help us. Is this so? In this case, it is said, our experience is of the inadequacy of words to deal with a certain situation. How is it different from the experience of surprise or embarrassment etc. when, having invited some important person to dinner at a restaurant, you discover an inadequacy of funds? We can describe this situation without actually mentioning the size of the bill or the amount of money you have with you. All that is relevant is the gap between them. Can we not similarly describe at least part of the experience of horror in terms of a gap between one's linguistically based interpretative competence and the object, scene, feeling or situation by which one is confronted? Surely a temporary local speechlessness is a quite ordinary matter that no more poses a threat to description than a swarm of flies of an indeterminable magnitude poses a threat to the number system.

It is worth considering how someone who believes that experience can pose an insuperable obstacle to language would react to this last example, because it raises an interesting point of principle. They might reply as follows: there is an absolute difference between running out of money and running out of words. Your meal is what it is whether or not you can pay for it, but the experience you cannot describe remains in a kind of ontological limbo. Put another way, not being able to pay for something does not affect it in itself, whereas not being able to describe it is a quite extraordinary event. One might after all begin to question whether it really existed, something one would never do to a safely consumed meal, still heavy on the stomach. And more importantly it is perverse to suppose that language can deal with something by labelling it 'another one of those indescribable things'. To recognize a difficulty is not to solve it. Finally the fact that such experiences may be transitory and personal and dependent upon the peculiar cognitive apparatus of individuals in no way reduces their importance. (To those who identify importance with universality, the reply would be that the transitory, the personal, the idiosyncratic *are* universal!) We would think it odd if a psychologist set up an experiment in which he tested the patience of hundreds of people, and because they each lost their patience at a different point concluded that patience was not real or objective. Similarly, the limits of language may appear in different experiences to different people without the reality of those limits being open to doubt. For we are not dealing with a wall or any other place, point or line that people ought to be able to agree to locate on a common map.

The discussion of the limits posed to linguistic description by experience has not so far concerned itself with religious, and particularly mystical, experience. I shall try to rectify this a little later on when I discuss theoretically the possibilities of using discursive strategies to overcome the apparent danger of being reduced to silence. I would now like to take up a suggestion made above that there might be logical limits to language. What is so important about this suggestion is that it offers a way of thinking about these limits which has at first sight nothing to do with the idea of realms too complex, rich, subtle, distant, etc. to describe. And indeed, it even offers the faint hope of being able to account for such fantasies. With these questions we turn our attention to Wittgenstein and Heidegger and a number of other philosophers. For here I think we find again that the limits of language depend on the formal limitations of description and not on the existence of an unspeakable realm.

II

There is a general argument, with interestingly different variants, of the following form: any language, or particular conceptual framework, rests on certain presuppositions which cannot be made explicit within that language. (It is like saying that one cannot see the ground one is standing on: the fact that we are standing on it means that it is hidden from view.) However the obvious response to this analogy is to say that one can always move one's feet. Perhaps a closer analogy would be trying to paint the floor one is standing on, without treading on another bit of painted floor. Interestingly one answer to this problem is to wait until the rest of the floor is dry, and that is precisely what a number of proponents of this view (Foucault, Gadamer) have said, that it is only through time (i.e. history) that the presuppositions of the present become visible and so discussable.

I have used a concrete example to introduce the structure of the problem because it is not otherwise easy to see what so many different accounts have in common. Let me mention a number of alternative formulations, those of Wittgenstein (in his *Tractatus Logico-Philosophicus* [hereafter *Tractatus*]), Heidegger, Gadamer, Kuhn, Foucault and Popper. In each case I will offer succinct accounts of the way in which for each of them this common structure gets articulated. Each of them recognizes the inaccessibility of presuppositions, and the role that some of our presuppositions play in making knowledge, thinking and language possible. But they each have different accounts of how inaccessible these presuppositions are, and whether the silence can be overcome. As we shall see, these differences may be accounted for by differences in the level at which 'language' etc. is being taken, so that the accounts are not necessarily incompatible. These different positions may be roughly grouped as follows. (1) That there are things that just cannot be said, ever. I attribute this view to the early Wittgenstein and to Heidegger. (2) That every overarching conceptual scheme rests on certain tacit assumptions that cannot be stated within that scheme, but which the subsequent course of intellectual history reveal. I attribute this view to Foucault, Gadamer and Kuhn. (3) That while it is true that general theories, ways of life, and ways of using language rest on tacit assumptions, nothing prevents us from changing our ground and becoming aware of them. This view I find in Popper. Let us look at these views in more detail.

At the end of his *Tractatus* [1921], Wittgenstein makes the famous remark, 'Of what we cannot speak we must remain silent.' There has been much ink spilled on the meaning of this sentence. Wittgenstein does make some fascinating remarks about ethics and metaphysics eight years later (1929), which I shall discuss shortly, but to understand this particular remark we need look no further than the problem of the position of logical form in the picture theory of language promulgated in the *Tractatus*. For Wittgenstein, language is reducible to elementary propositions which combine names together in ways that mirror the way objects in the world can be combined in atomic facts. And the complexity of the world can be resolved into such possible combinations of objects.

This is an account of how it is that language can describe the world, and it accentuates its descriptive functions. But it contains within it both a limitation on language, and the seeds of a paradox. The limitation appears in the following remark: 'propositions represent the whole of reality but they cannot represent what they must have in common with reality *in order to be able to* represent it – a logical form' (*Tractatus*, 2.18).

Wittgenstein is saying that propositions represent or picture facts – and facts are all *in* the world. So there cannot be a proposition about the relationship between propositions and the world, because that would not be a *fact in the world*. Now, Wittgenstein's words 'in order to be able to' (what propositions must have in common with reality *in order to be able to* represent it) allude to what are called transcendental questions, questions about how something that we all agree exists or is the case, is none the less possible. (The question here is: how is it possible that language represents or relates to the world?) And what he is doing is in fact denying the possibility of transcendental description. We cannot, he claims, use language to describe the conditions of possibility of language, or how language fundamentally relates to the world, because, as we have said, language can only represent or picture what is in the world, and its relation to the world is not in it, not a part of it. It is like saying that (ignoring mirrors and other reflecting surfaces, leaving 'tricks' to one side) a photographer can only take pictures of the world not of himself taking pictures of the world. But this formal limitation on language (as I called it earlier) also contains the seeds, if not the vigorous sprouts of a paradox, which is that these remarks, and indeed the whole of the *Tractatus*, are the very sort of remarks that Wittgenstein has claimed are not descriptive. And yet description is of the essence of his account of language. At the end of the *Tractatus* he compares the whole book to a ladder that we climb up only to discard when it has served its function. He supposes that what we cannot say in language can none the less be shown. And it is this showing that he is referring to when he talks about silence or being silent. Such a silence is logically tied to the activity of philosophizing. He is not insisting that we cease to speak altogether but that there is more to speech (or writing) than what is *said*. One way of putting it is to talk about what is *shown*.

A number of comments are in order here. First, it is dangerous to think of this as a mystical doctrine for we then pretend it cannot be understood at all. Many a serious philosophical endeavour bears witness to the problematic status of its own utterances. This can be made apparent without being said. Second, if we reject the picture theory of language (and many people, including Wittgenstein himself, do reject it) what becomes of the saying/showing distinction? Wittgenstein found a number of internal difficulties with the doctrine – how to deal with negative, hypothetical or counterfactual propositions, for example – but it also seemed to rest on a rigidly logical conception of language. It leads one to wonder whether his references to silence and to showing are not just symptoms of the narrowness of his theory of language.

Does not the need for a special 'showing' disappear as soon as we allow into language not just a picturing, descriptive function but also imaginative, rhetorical, poetic, associative functions too (and not just negatively included). The limits of language must surely depend on how one thinks of language. Wittgenstein in effect recognizes, when he talks of showing, that language can do more than he ought to be able to allow, but he could not thematize it within the framework of the *Tractatus*.

I mentioned above in passing his remarks on ethics, and now I must briefly elaborate them as I have generalized the force of his remarks to cover the possibility of any transcendental description, that is, any philosophical discourse that thought it had a special subject matter, or domain of facts not part of the world. These remarks show again, quite clearly, that the limits of language are intimately connected to the limits of one's understanding of it or of one's ability to deploy it. I quote (from Wittgenstein):

I can readily think what Heidegger means by Being and Angst. Man has the impulse to run up against the limits of language. Think, for example, of the astonishment that anything exists. This astonishment cannot be expressed in the form of a question, and there is also no answer to it. Everything which we feel like saying can, a priori, only be nonsense. Nevertheless, we do run up against the limits of language[3] (Michael Murray [ed.], *Heidegger and Modern Philosophy*, p. 80)

Consider what Wittgenstein says here, that the wonder of existence cannot be expressed in the form of a question. Clearly this is only true if one means by 'question' something of a logically approved form (that is, something to which one can imagine the shape of a possible answer, which would itself have to be an empirical proposition). For people have been expressing their wonder in the form of a question for ages. Heidegger asks, for example, 'Why is there anything rather than nothing?' And shortly after our quotation above, Wittgenstein goes on: 'the tendency to thrust points towards something', which perhaps oddly[4] he calls ethics. In doing so, he connects up nonsense with showing and with silence. This kind of nonsense is a logical silence (that is, from a logical point of view one is 'saying nothing') but what it shows or points to is of enormous importance.

Wittgenstein's strict understanding of a 'question' confirms our opinion that views about the limits of language seem to follow rather directly from views about what language 'is'. A comparison of Heidegger's way of thinking about questions might help here. For Heidegger, the kind of metaphysical questions that Wittgenstein calls *important nonsense* are not there to be answered (they are not factual questions) but rather they 'open up a path of thinking', as he would put it. The positivist might reply that the question is empty and that Heidegger is leading us up the garden path. But in fact Heidegger does not take such questions at their face value. He tries to make sense of the fact that we ask such questions without relegating them to expressing some irrational urge. Heidegger's understanding of questioning involves a significantly richer understanding of language than that offered by Wittgenstein, and in consequence leads to a rather different understanding of the limits of language than Wittgenstein's. We should retain from Wittgenstein an extreme caution in interpreting that philosophical discourse which takes the form of descriptions of transcendental realities. But we need not take the ultimate precaution of silence, and there is a lot more to philosophical discourse than showing.

Heidegger himself also offers us a strong account of the limits of language, strangely oscillating between a parallel with and a contrast to that of Wittgenstein. I will try to bring out this strange relation by quoting one or two short passages from his writings. I will start with a few lines from near the end of a lecture, 'Time and Being' (1962), which echoes the end of the *Tractatus*.

> To all appearances, all this says nothing. It does indeed say nothing as long as we hear a mere sentence in what was said, and expose the sentence to the cross-examination of logic. But what if (instead) we take what was said and adopt it unceasingly as the guide for our thinking? (p. 24)

And at the beginning of this lecture he wrote

> Let me give a little hint on how to listen. The point is not to listen to a series of propositions, but rather to follow the movement of showing. (p. 2)

Wittgenstein's distinction was between saying and showing. Heidegger distinguishes speaking and saying. In another essay, 'The Way to Language', he puts his distinction like this:

> To say and to speak are not identical. A man may speak, speak endlessly, and all the time say nothing. Another man may remain silent, not speak at all and yet without speaking, say a great deal ... 'Say' means to show, to let appear, to let be seen and heard.[5]

So whereas for Wittgenstein showing is something that goes beyond mere saying, the mere uttering of propositions, for Heidegger that 'uttering of propositions', would be called speaking, and in order actually to say something one would have to do more, to 'show' something. But behind these terminological variations, a similar distinction is being made between the uttering of propositions, and the further possibility of giving voice to something, bringing something out, or making something clear. The difference is not between uttering certain words and communicating something to someone else (there is clearly another important disinction here) but between uttering certain words and saying them in such a way that their significance stands out.

The major difference between the early Wittgenstein and Heidegger is that for Wittgenstein the essence of language, its primary function, is picturing, representing, describing the world. Showing is an additional possibility predicated on the descriptive function. For Heidegger, on the other hand, when language is used in this descriptive, information-conveying role, it is being reduced to a mere instrument. Before we can use language to convey information, it is language that brings to light the variety of things in the world and, just as importantly, the different ways things are. It is language that makes it possible to think of possibilities, values, qualities, relations, complex tenses and moods. But there is a temptation to think that relations, qualities, etc. are just different kinds of 'objects'. This danger is a consequence of the predominance of a certain way of using (and taking) language, which he calls objectifying, that is, descriptive, propositional language. Heidegger opposes to this another way of using language which he calls non-objectifying. To use language in a non-objectifying way is to show what cannot just be stated, to point to something without directly describing it, to allow something to appear without slapping a label on it.

For Wittgenstein, the world is a collection of facts (which propositions ideally depict). For Heidegger, this model is just the reflection of an objectifying way of thinking. What Heidegger tries to do is to handle language in such a way that the uttering of descriptive propositions occurs as one possibility among others. In his early *magnum opus* *Being and Time* the name he gave to the space in which such multiple possibilities unfold was *existence*.

Now, as I write, I wonder whether what I am saying about Heidegger's understanding of language is at all helpful, whether anything is getting across. Suppose that my account here is difficult to get hold of. It could be my fault, that I have been too cursory, or that I myself do not fully understand it. It could be Heidegger's fault, that he succumbed to what Gilbert Ryle, in an early review of *Being and Time*, predicted would be a 'windy mysticism', or that Heidegger has simply become entangled in his own words. But it could be that the very form of my account accentuates a difficulty inherent in the subject matter. For I am trying to give an account of something – Heidegger's understanding of language and its limits – which is itself framed in opposition to just such a possibility of giving an account of something, that is, giving a description of it, as an adequate story about what is going on in language. After all, Heidegger spends much of his later writing trying to induce his readers to have what he calls 'a new experience with language'. And just as Wittgenstein said that the reader who had not had his thoughts would not be able to understand the *Tractatus*, Heidegger too tries to bring his reader to his way of seeing language by all sorts of means. And all I have given are the bare bones of an account.

In the essay cited above ('The way to language') he writes, 'Everything spoken stems in a variety of ways from the unspoken, whether this be something not yet spoken, or whether it be what must remain unspoken in the sense that it is beyond the reach of speaking.' If Ryle's judgement ('windy mysticism') were correct, we would have to think of this *beyond* the reach of speaking as something that transcends the mundane level of ordinary life and experience. Yet Heidegger is resolutely opposed to such an idea. He says elsewhere that 'we do not want to get anywhere. We would like only, for once, to get to just where we are already.'[6] What is unspoken, and it may at times be necessarily unspoken, is what cannot be revealingly stated in a propositional form, or cannot be so stated without producing an essential distortion. This can be very simple, and very close to home. For Wittgenstein it was 'the ethical', and for Heidegger, perhaps, 'existence'. It is this insight that the limits of language are not outer limits, but *limits that appear, and may indeed be overcome, within language* that gives these philosophers their extraordinary interest. Wittgenstein's later interest in the variety of ways of using language complements Heidegger's interest in the poetic, evocative uses of language. It remains true, however, that Heidegger holds on to the belief in privileged, insightful, revealing ways of using language, whereas Wittgenstein dissolves the idea that language has limits in the diversity of language games. What I would fasten on here is the fact that both of these philosophers talk about silence, even recommend it in various ways, and yet move away from the frame of reference within which actual silence would be called for, and develop ways of carrying on speaking and writing. We ought perhaps to be less dismissive of those mystics who say in book after book that nothing can be said. I shall return to this question shortly.

In the last quotation from Heidegger, he made a distinction between what is not yet spoken and what must remain unspoken. This points to what could be called the moderate position on silence – that there are some things that cannot be said now – at this time in history. I will now try to discuss this claim succinctly, at some risk of distortion.

III

Both Foucault[7] and Gadamer[8] are engaged in a kind of philosophy involving the interpretation of history, which British philosophers have too often left to historians. Hegel offered a complete account of world history as the progress of reason, or the development of spirit towards absolute self-knowledge, and influenced both the Marxist and the idealist traditions in nineteenth-century Britain, each of which took history very seriously. Yet official histories are not wholly inaccurate in diagnosing the rise of twentieth-century positivism, logical atomism, and then linguistic philosophy, as the virtual eclipse of historical perspective within influential philosophical circles. (Collingwood was a late and prestigious exception.) The interpretation of history was often regarded as something of an intellectual swamp, in which anyone with any ambition would soon contract the fever known as 'metaphysics', encouraging at best an analytical study of the conceptual tools of historical understanding. Foucault and Gadamer – two very different philosophers – are each quite as concerned with the problems of theory and method in historical interpretation, but they also engage in its practice as well.

Now one of the obvious problems of any philosophical treatment of history, and especially of the history of ideas, or of the history of philosophy, is that the first lesson one learns is that one is dealing with a succession of people who thought that what they said was true quite independently of the time at which they said it. And yet the frames of reference they adopted (their conceptual schemes, their theories, even their basic assumptions about the shape of knowledge) – things which seem so self-evident to them that they may not even be visible as assumptions – these change from epoch to epoch. And moreover the judgement that these changes have some sort of order to them (such that they might, for example, embody progress) is itself a view that is rather too easily assigned to the nineteenth century.

Both Foucault and Gadamer conclude that our most basic assumptions (for example, about the nature of knowledge, about the relation between language and the world, about the division between madness and reason) always constitute a layer which is, if you like, structurally invisible, and which we cannot make explicit at the time. Gadamer talks of these as prejudgements, Foucault of an *episteme*, that is, a fundamental cognitive structure. At this level of generality we could include Thomas Kuhn's idea of a *paradigm*,[9] which might perhaps be glossed as a fundamental frame of reference underlying a number of scientific theories and practices at a given period. In each case we have a limit to what can be said, thought, understood, communicated, even noticed. It is a limit to language if language here is understood as the totality of available procedures for observation, interpretation, description and explanation. What each of these accounts recognizes is that there have been enormous and dramatic shifts in these webs of comprehension, shifts which in a real sense are thinkable as at best empty possibilities from within the webs themselves.

A simple argument underlies the claim that one cannot think let alone talk about these fundamental assumptions. We do not have to resort to the language of archaeology or psychoanalysis and say they are 'too deeply buried'. They are, as I have said, structurally invisible, just as one's eyes are, in that one can never see them directly. The argument is this: in order to scrutinize these assumptions, in order to question them, doubt them, even note them as assumptions, one would have to make use of the established procedures for noting, questioning, scrutinizing, doubting, etc. And yet it is in such established procedures that the assumptions lie. So the attempt to bring them to light would only confirm them. Obviously this is an oversimple picture, and it does not explain how historical change is possible. But it has the consequence that the basic epistemological principles on which an epoch is founded are only visible after they have ceased to function in a foundational role. If as Kuhn claimed the periods of transition (which he called periods of 'revolutionary science', and for which Foucault's equivalent would be transformations of an *episteme*) are rare, the personal attempt to bring one's most basic assumptions to light will only be rewarded accidentally – if one happens to be riding on the crest of a historical wave.

Popper offers a third alternative to what we could call the strong thesis of Wittgenstein and Heidegger, and the moderate thesis of Foucault, Gadamer and Kuhn: that there is nothing that we cannot at will reflect on and make explicit. I am thinking of the thesis he calls in a number of places 'the myth of the framework'. He describes this myth as 'the central bulwark of irrationalism' and says 'it exaggerates a difficulty into an impossibility'. Let me quote the crucial paragraph:

> I do admit that at any moment we are prisoners caught in the framework of our theories, our expectations, our past experiences, our language. But we are prisoners in a Pickwickian sense: if we try, we can break out of our framework at any time. Admittedly, we shall find ourselves again in a framework but it will be a better and roomier one, and we can at any moment break out of it again. The central point is that a critical discussion and a comparison of the various frameworks is always possible.[10]

What is interesting here is that Popper accepts what I have called the structural invisibility of those principles that constitute 'the framework'. But he is claiming that this applies only while one is actually making use of the framework. For one can always stand back and reflect on one's basic frame of reference.

The attitude lying behind these remarks is not wholly implausible. If he expressed it more moderately, for example, that belief in an inaccessible framework is no reason for not trying or bothering to reflect on our assumptions, it would surely be sound advice. As it stands, however, it is quite unrealistic to suppose that one can at any time change one's frame of reference just by reflection. And when he says we always end up in a roomier space, it sounds like a recipe for almost miraculous progress. And Popper's references to the 'rational', to 'critical discussion', to intellectual and scientific progress (ever roomier spaces) seem themselves to belong to an era of confidence in the power of science that has passed. One wonders how far it is possible for Popper himself to become aware of the fundamental conditions on which his own enterprise rests. Foucault, for instance, in the preface to *Madness and Civilization*, claims that our concept of reason and rationality is a product of a historical distancing from unreason, from madness, and a silencing of the dialogue there once was between reason and unreason. The language and practice of psychiatry has given the name of science to this subjugation. This history cannot be justified in the name of reason, for it serves to constitute reason as such.

Perhaps most importantly, Popper's claim raises the vital question whether we might not be dealing, both here and in the cases of Foucault, Gadamer and Kuhn, with a number of distinct levels of framework, theory, conceptual scheme, etc. Certainly a good scientist ought to be able to construct and abandon hypotheses pretty much at will, just as a detective would in trying to solve a crime. The detective would both test out existing hypotheses and try to develop new ones in case the first ones came to a dead end. But there is a difference between the conceptual underpinnings of a scientific theory or even a collection of such theories; basic views about what constitutes knowledge; and the variable importance of epistemological standards of knowledge and 'truth' in regulating our discourse.

Arguably, Popper is dealing with the first; Kuhn, Foucault and Gadamer with the second; and Wittgenstein and Heidegger with the last. If so it suggests that the question of the limits of language does not only depend on one's theory of language, as I have already suggested, but, when one is dealing with these forms of structural invisibility, it depends crucially on the level at which the 'framework', or whatever one wants to call it, is conceived.

IV

In the last part of this chapter I would like to turn back to the original question: whether there is such a thing as necessary silence, whether one can ever reach a point at which there is still something to be said, while it is impossible to say it. I want to argue that silence literally understood is never forced upon us. Or, at least, that philosophical progress consists in the development of complex strategies of reading, writing and speaking, rather than the delineation of fields of necessary silence.

In focusing on the question of necessary silence I am returning to the concerns of Wittgenstein and Heidegger because it is from their perspective that the further concern with philosophical style and strategy as a way of getting round silence arises. For Foucault, Gadamer, Kuhn and Popper, all that is needed is a certain critical vigilance, and a certain care in avoiding concepts belonging to frameworks one rejects.

I hope I will also be able to give some inkling as to why certain continental philosophers are difficult. They are difficult not because they have chosen to shelter in the thickets of obscurity as a protection against the onslaughts of open public debate, but because they are responding to what they perceive as the limits of a certain kind of language, a certain way of using language.

The historical connection between philosophical and religious writing is extremely strong. We pride ourselves today on having freed philosophy from this connection. I will not contest this here.[11] But the response of many to the doctrines of Wittgenstein and Heidegger has been to label them mystical, which would suggest that they have regressed, historically speaking. In my view, one of the most important and interesting ways in which philosophy has developed away from theology is in its attempts to handle the questions of the limits of knowledge, of reason, of language ... without positing a higher realm and indeed without positing another realm at all. Kant's wavering between positive and negative ways of understanding the noumenon – the world in so far as it transcends our phenomenal and experiential grasp of it – could be seen as a kind of threshold of the modern era. And it is precisely because both Wittgenstein and Heidegger confront this very issue of the limits of language without positing another realm at all that their enterprise is a philosophical one and not a displaced or misplaced theology.

As I have said, each of them sees the limits of language to be dependent on a certain use of language, which we could call descriptive, and they attempt to show how these limits might be negotiated by using language in other ways. These two doctrines are not mystical, but it is, none the less, fascinating to see that this decision to opt for a novel linguistic strategy (and not merely the poetic and evocative sort) was anticipated by mysticism. I am thinking of the 'negative theology' of the pseudo-Dionysus. His thinking has an affirmative as well as a negative phase, and the negative prepares us for the affirmative, in which he does indeed engage in transcendental description. In the negative phase however he attempts to use negative statements as a way of avoiding the misleading banalities of direct affirmative description. He says of the 'first cause' that

> He is not soul, or intelligence,
> not word,
> not said, not thought,
> not powerful, not power,
> not knowledge, not truth,
> not kingship, not wisdom,
> not a being, not a nonbeing,
> not definable, not nameable,
> not knowable,
> not affirmable, not deniable,
> etc. etc.
>
> (*The Mystical Theology*)[12]

Once he has established that no empirical predicates can be successfully applied to God, he goes on to make certain affirmative claims (despite the last line we have quoted) about a transcendental realm, which make his writing religious rather than philosophical. But what remains of interest is his attempt to use a succession of negations as a way of conveying something that straightforward description could not convey, or at least to prepare the way for understanding his subsequent higher level affirmations. He is weaseling his way round what must first have appeared as the need for silence. For philosophers for whom transcendental description is no longer an option, the burden on linguistic style and strategy is even heavier. Let me first mention some of the strategies that philosophers have explored. I will say a few more words about Wittgenstein and Heidegger, and add to the list Kierkegaard and Derrida.

Wittgenstein: (a) at the end of the *Tractatus* he asks us to take up a certain attitude to each of the propositions in the book he has just finished. To help us take up this attitude he offers an analogy: treat the book as a ladder you can dispense with after climbing it. The book itself in no way prepares us for this. His strategy here is to ask us to do the work of overcoming the limits of language by taking his words in a certain way, a displaced reading.

(b) The *Philosophical Investigations* on the other hand immerses the reader in the complex and varied ways in which we use language. That descriptive use of language which seems to be responsible for the experience of its limits is treated as one language game among others. The dramatic generalizations by which philosophers traditionally generate their paradoxes are dissolved or replaced by careful investigations of the way words like 'justification', 'explanation', 'mean', 'perceive', 'naming', actually function in our language. The moral is: if the problem of the limits of language arises within language, perhaps the solution lies there too.

Heidegger: we could easily say of the later Wittgenstein what Heidegger said of his own writing, that the point is not to get anywhere (else) but (for once) to get to where we are already, that is, in language. He does not mean to liken us to bookworms but to say (and, again, the later Wittgenstein would have agreed) that we cannot separate our 'world' or our 'existence' from the manifold linguistic practices in which we engage. And when we think of language as essentially descriptive, and as a means for conveying information, we distort our understanding of the 'world' and our 'existence' in it. This is why he aims at bringing us to a 'new experience with language'. The strategies he employs here are manifold.

He plays with etymology – not always to the satisfaction of scholars – with the aim of alerting us to language not just as a means but as a witness to our *dwelling* in it; he distorts ordinary syntax, using, for example, philosophical tautology (the world worlds, nothing noths), category mistakes (language speaks); he is terminologically innovative, giving to complex expressions (e.g. Being-in-the-world) a primitive status and allowing words that have had little previous philosophical usage to bear a heavy weight (care, opening, preserving, resoluteness ...); he crosses out words he uses, leaving both the word and the crossing out, especially with Being; he gives careful philosophical readings of German philosophical poets – Rilke, Hölderlin, George, Trakl – who have themselves taken the limits of language as their concern; like Wittgenstein, he tells us how to read what he has written and how not to.

In brief, when we read Heidegger we will be most rewarded if we see his difficulty as a positive response to the problem of the limits of an objectifying mode of writing.[13]

Kierkegaard: as is well known, Kierkegaard adopted numerous pseudonyms to bear a whole range of philosophical and religious standpoints. There are few literary genres he did not explore with a view to explaining himself better. For Kierkegaard, as we see in Chapter 6, 'Indirect Communication', the central truth which philosophy usually overlooks is the subjectivity of the individual, and by subjectivity he means not just one's inner life of private thoughts, but the fact of one's peculiar involvement in and responsibility for those thoughts. At a particularly interesting point in his *Concluding Unscientific Postscript* he argues quite straightforwardly that subjectivity cannot be communicated. But this is soon changed into the claim that it cannot be communicated directly and very soon we find that actually the only true communication is indirect. He contrasts this indirect communication (using metaphor, parables, irony, etc.), in which one's subjectivity is evidenced but not stated, with ordinary direct communication in which, he claims, one is not really giving anything of oneself, and so not truly communicating. The example he gives is of tender and incomplete feelings of love for another. He claims that to state one's feelings is to transform them. Making them public – that kind of objectification – really does change things. To state one's feelings towards someone to that very person is to arouse expectations, to solicit similar feelings, etc. Moreover, it is, in his view, to change a dynamic process of the transformation of one's feelings into something fixed and completed. To repeat, the only way round this cluster of problems that would otherwise lead one to silence or blundering is, he claims, indirect communication, and this is indeed what he practises.

I have tried to show that the limits of language can be seen as 'internal' to language, as the limits of description, rather than a barrier separating us from esoteric knowledge of a higher realm. I have also tried to show that if silence seems called for initially, it is usually if not always possible to develop and exploit other ways of using language instead.

I would like, in conclusion, to suggest something further, which sometimes seems obvious, and sometimes profound. It is that the sense and significance of there being something that cannot be said is itself an effect of language. We who use language (and not just we philosophers) do often treat description as the paradigm of language use. What then seems closed or resistant to description then takes on a value which has often been thought of as transcendent, as beyond our ken. It is not that language cannot handle the transcendent. Rather the transcendent is the name we give to the discovery of the limits of descriptive language, tacitly but erroneously supposing that it names a realm that cannot be described. If this is so, then it is not surprising that if we expand our understanding of the functions of language, our sense of there being such a realm will disappear.

Notes

1 This is of course a central problem for Kant's understanding of the noumenal in his first Critique.
2 I mention this fantastic desire in Chapter 8, 'Performative Reflexivity'.
3 It is worth mentioning here that when this was first translated, the opening reference to Heidegger was entirely deleted, as if Wittgenstein needed protecting from his own interest in Heidegger (or was it the British public that needed protecting from the knowledge of this interest?).
4 It is nothing like so odd if you consider the way Kierkegaard used the word ethics. And he is without doubt a strong influence here.
5 In *On The Way to Language* [1959], trans. P. Hertz (New York: Harper & Row, 1971), p. 122.
6 *Poetry Language Thought*, trans. A. Hofstadter (New York: Harper & Row, 1971), p. 190.
7 See his *Madness and Civilization* [1961], trans. R. Howard (London: Tavistock, 1967); *The Order of Things* [1966] (London: Tavistock, 1970); *Discipline and Punish* [1975] (London: Allen Lane, 1977); and *The History of Sexuality* [1976] (London: Peregrine, 1987).
8 See, for example, *Truth and Method* [2nd edn 1965] (London: Sheed & Ward, 1975).
9 See his *The Structure of Scientific Revolutions* (Chicago: University of Chicago Press, 1970).

10 See his 'Normal Science and Its Dangers', in I. Lakatos and A. Musgrave (eds), *Criticism and the Growth of Knowledge* (Cambridge: Cambridge University Press, 1970), p. 56.

11 Others have contested this supposed separation. Consider Nietzsche's 'We have not got rid of God if we still believe in grammar' (*Twilight of the Idols* [1889], trans. R. J. Hollingdale [Harmondsworth: Penguin, 1968]) or Derrida's 'The age of the sign is essentially...theological. Perhaps it will never end' (*Of Grammatology*, trans G. C. Spivak [Baltimore: Johns Hopkins, 1974], p. 14.)

12 The pseudo-Dionysus is so-called because he was not the Dionysus (= Dennis) who converted St Paul in the 1st century. He probably lived in the sixth century in Syria, though no one is sure.

13 See my *The Deconstruction of Time* (Atlantic Highlands: Humanities, 1989), Part 4, Chapter 3 ('The Question of Strategy'), pp. 293–319.

Further reading

The adequation of language to experience, at least in principle, is a presumption of the phenomenology of Husserl, and clear statements of this position can be found in his *Ideas* [1913], trans. Boyce Gibson (London: George Allen & Unwin, 1931), especially Section 66. Also his *Formal and Transcendental Logic* [1929], trans. D. Cairns (The Hague: Nijhoff, 1969), especially Sections 1–4, as well as his *Experience and Judgement* [1939], trans. J. Churchill and K. Ameriks (Evanston: Northwestern, 1973).

For accounts of 'experiences' that unsettle this assurance, Sartre's *Nausea* [1938], trans. R. Baldick (Harmondsworth: Penguin, 1965), pp. 175 ff is a classic source. See also Kierkegaard's *The Concept of Dread* and *Fear and Trembling*, *The Sickness unto Death*, all translated by Walter Lowrie and published by Princeton; Jaspers' account of 'Limit-Situations' in his *Psychology of World Views* [Berlin: Springer, 1931], translated in part in Maurice Friedman (ed.), *The Worlds of Existentialism* [Chicago: University of Chicago Press, 1964], pp. 100–1); and Heidegger's treatment of Dread in his 'What is Metaphysics' [1929] in *Basic Writings*, ed. David Krell (London: Harper & Row, 1977).

For discussion of the difference between deconstruction and negative theology the best source is Derrida's 'Comment ne pas parler' in his *Psyché. Inventions de l'autre* (Paris: Galilée, 1987). Heidegger's 'Phenomenology and theology' in *The Piety of Thinking* (Bloomington: Indiana University Press, 1976) provides useful background. Susan Handelman's 'Jacques Derrida and the heretic hermeneutic', in Mark Krupnik (ed.), *Displacement: Derrida and After*, (Bloomington: Indiana, 1982) is very useful. Mark Taylor's *Erring: A Postmodern A/theology* (Chicago: University of Chicago Press, 1984) provides an original perspective.

2

Metaphysics and metaphor

Philosophy is said to have taken the 'linguistic turn' in this century. One hundred years ago, a philosopher would think in terms of mind, spirit, experience, consciousness; now the by-word is language.[1] This is of course an oversimplication. But it is oversimple not just because concepts like 'experience' and 'consciousness' are still alive, but also because the linguistic turn is not a single-stranded phenomenon. What do positivism, ordinary language philosophy, speech-act theory, semiology, structuralism, hermeneutics, post-structuralism all have in common other than their indebtedness to an association of philosophy with some aspect of language? No doubt the proper answer to this is quite complex. But there are a few smaller movements within the larger turn worth tracing out.

First, with Frege, early Husserl, early Wittgenstein and Carnap, the concept of language employed by philosophy was essentially what Derrida calls *logocentric*. Its basic dimensions are displayed in such logical functions as judgement, assertion and representation. On a second model, reflected in the shift in Wittgenstein's own writing, in the appearance of ordinary language philosophy in the 1950s and later with the development of speech-act theory and pragmatics (Austin, Grice, Searle) the basic conception of language became contextualist and pragmatic. For Wittgenstein, for example, language could only be understood within a 'form of life'. But there is a third position, one which understands language essentially through those possibilities of relatively autonomous development opened up by literature, poetry, and indeed texts in general. Here we would include semiology, structuralism, hermeneutics and post-structuralism (Saussure, Barthes, Derrida, Ricoeur). In this simple schematism, the linguistic turn focuses first on logic, then life, and finally literature. One way of taking this last step, while remaining at least in touch with philosophy, is to ride with Heidegger and Derrida. An important strand in the recent explosion

26

of interest in metaphor is linked historically with the last move.[2] The ultimate aim of this chapter will be to show how this move affects the way we read and think about philosophy.

The reassessment of the relationship between philosophy and metaphor in the English-speaking world was precipitated by many different factors. Here I would single out three: the demise of the logocentric view of language, language thought of as (literally) picturing reality; the breakdown of procedures for deciding on the metaphorical/literal claims made during periods of philosophical/theoretical transition from one frame of reference to another; the translation of Heidegger's later writings and those of Derrida, each of which resist an interpretation within the familiar literal/metaphorical opposition.

Consider first the demise of the logocentric view of language This does not automatically focus special attention on the status of metaphor. But the concept of metaphor is part of a way of understanding language left without a real job to do after the displacement of the logocentric model. This way of understanding language takes for granted a rigid distinction between literal and figurative uses of language. And with the disappearance of the belief that language pictures the world or directly represents it, the merely *derivative* status of metaphor is threatened. It is no longer at all obvious that metaphorical claims are to be treated either as literally false, or, more charitably, as disguised forms of literal utterance, into which they should be retranslated. Metaphor becomes problematic.

A second factor precipitating a reassessment of the place of metaphor in philosophy is the recognition that at least some claims about the proper relationship between concepts (such as Ryle's claim that some statements embody 'category mistakes') are not eternal truths, but rather prescriptive reflections of the constitutive semantic order of certain language games. Once we recognize that these games can change then there will be transitional periods (in science, but also in everyday discourse) in which it will often be unclear whether an utterance is to be taken metaphorically or literally, because no clear categorical structure is available. Put briefly, category instability in transition from one frame of reference to another threatens the distinction between the metaphorical and the literal. (A version of this thesis is to be found in Rorty's book *Philosophy and the Mirror of Nature*.)

The third source of disturbance to an assured philosophical understanding of metaphor can be found in the appearance of translations of Heidegger's later writings which try to open up for the reader 'a new experience with language'. On a surface inspection these texts seem to be riddled with metaphor. Somewhat differently, but also contributing to what we might call the 'liberation of metaphor' Derrida destabilizes any conceptual or categorical schema by arguing for an underlying and ultimately uncontrollable *play of differences*, a play not subject to rules like a game, but one which threatens any neat semantic ordering, and so threatens the distinction between the literal and the figurative. Much more could be said here; I hope this is enough to set the scene.

In exploring the field thus opened up the central concern will not be with the nature of the metaphor, nor the theory of metaphor, but with the role played by metaphor (and our concepts of metaphor) in the understanding, and practice of philosophy. (I should also add that I use 'metaphor' here in the broad sense that includes rather than distinguishes itself from other figurative modes, such as metonymy and synecdoche.) Consider first the simple solution to the problem of philosophy's entanglement with metaphor: the elimination of metaphor.

The purity thesis

The purity thesis is the thesis that philosophy can and must dispense with metaphor to realize its goal of rational clarity.

This thesis appears at different times in different garb. I would distinguish three different forms it has taken, ontological, epistemological and, roughly speaking, 'discursive'.

After Aristotle's great labours, philosophers have often taken it for granted that there are different categories of stuff in the world, different kinds of beings. This is no simple empirical discovery, but the product of real conceptual/analytical labour. A philosophical discourse which recognized this and built on it would govern itself by an understanding of which words were proper to what things. It would not for example think it made sense to talk of thoughts as located in space. Infringements of such rules would surely lead to error, and what Ryle called category mistakes would be cases of such errors.[3] Metaphor feeds on and exploits just such categorial confusion; it brings together beings that should be kept apart. Metaphor, in short, is a threat to categorial order, and hence to philosophy, in so far as philosophy requires, presupposes or is directed towards such an order.

An epistemological argument for such a thesis can be found in Locke: '[words] interpose themselves so much between our understandings and the truth which it would contemplate and apprehend that, like the *medium* through which visible objects pass, their obscurity and disorder does not seldom cast a mist before our eyes and impose upon our understandings'.[4]

Like Hobbes, Locke attributes this obscuring of knowledge to the figurative use of language. This is perfectly all right for what he calls the *civil* use of words but not for the *philosophical*, which is 'a use of words such as may serve to convey the precise nature of things'. Another epistemological source of the purity argument is obviously Descartes. What is central to knowledge is the clarity and distinctness of our ideas. Metaphor only endangers this clarity. And finally the purity thesis appears as a claim about the need for philosophical discourse to free itself from the figurative.

Figurative language has always been thought of as threatening the value of clarity. Metaphorical expressions, taken literally, are false. When we probe them more deeply we find indeterminacy and vagueness. Philosophy on the other hand is a conceptual form of thought. Metaphor is also a threat to reason. As Susan Stebbing says 'an argument derived from a metaphor will be a bad one'.[5] For metaphors work on similarity, but in some sense everything is similar to everything else. Philosophy requires identity and sameness, not merely the empirical relation of similarity.

The reference to Susan Stebbing is important as proof, if proof were needed, that the purity thesis cannot be thought of as abandoned in the seventeenth and eighteenth centuries. In fact it had a new burst of life with the logical positivism of the 1930s. What is central to that doctrine is a theory of verification which insists that meaningful utterances can be cashed out in direct experience. Figurative language has meaning only in so far as it can be given a literal translation, and it is more usually responsible for those misuses of language that generate philosophical error. Positivism combined an epistemological argument with a semantic argument, much in the same way as Locke and Hobbes had done. And in much the same way it saw progress in philosophy resulting from the purging of philosophical language, or, in our metaphor, its purification.

It is not surprising that the typical ways of understanding metaphor itself – the comparison and substitutive models – both involve the claim that metaphor is nothing but literal utterance with emotive decoration.

The meaningful core of a metaphor is revealed by translating it back into its literal origins. On the comparison theory, for example, to say that 'old age is the evening of life' is to say that evening and old age are similar in certain respects, although not in others. On this view metaphors are really similes which can be eliminated by translating into simile and specifying the similarity.

The purity thesis typically combines two claims: the *desirability* for philosophy of having clean tools, a language that reflects reality and employs clearly defined concepts; and the *possibility* of eliminating the figurative from rational discourse.

The return of metaphor

But whatever we think about the desirability of purifying language for philosophical purposes, is it in fact possible? A resounding negative answer would announce the *return of metaphor*. In our first example this return takes the form of revenge. I am thinking of Nietzsche's account in his early essay 'Truth and Falsity in Their Ultramoral Sense' and the account put forward by Polyphilos in Anatole France's *The Garden of Epicurus*.[6] The Nietzsche essay is well known, and known best through an often-quoted paragraph. I will not miss the opportunity to quote it again. It comes after an account of the intellect as the creator of useful illusions.

> What therefore is truth? A mobile army of metaphors, metonymies, anthropomorphisms; in short a sum of human relations which became poetically and rhetorically intensified, metamorphosed, adorned, and after long usage seem fixed, canonic and binding; truths are illusions of which one has forgotten that they *are* illusions; worn-out metaphors which have become powerless to affect the senses, coins which have their obverse effaced and now are no longer of account as coins but merely as metal.[7]

Nietzsche's argument for this view, if one reconstructs it, is that the most primitive contact we have with the world – through sensations – shows the things in the world to be of infinite complexity. And yet we pick them out in language only via certain particular features they have. Only in this way can we have classes and categories of things to which to apply general words. But in picking on those features of things by which they are similar to other things, and grasping them linguistically through those similarities, is not the basic move of language metaphorical? Nietzsche convinces himself that it is, and that the concept of truth (understood, as it commonly is, as representation) is a kind of compounding of an original metaphor.

But Nietzsche is clearly not just talking about truth, but about philosophy as a whole, as the 'purveyor of truth', the guardian of reason. For his criticism of 'truths' as 'worn-out metaphors which have become powerless to affect the senses' is a claim one can make about the ideality of all philosophical concepts, that they are dead metaphors – indeed it is just what Polyphilos says in the second example. The other way in which Nietzsche is clearly generalizing is in the phrase 'A mobile army of metaphors, metonymies, anthropomorphisms'. What this rightly suggests is that in philosophy the claim of truth is underpinned by a whole system of concepts and values, not just the single concept of truth in the abstract. Consider, for example, the idea of purity, as in Kant's *Critique of Pure Reason*; or rigour, in Husserl's 'Philosophy as a rigorous science'; or clarity (to describe style), the language of vision and light (insight, enlightenment, 'seeing' what is meant . . .), the language of grasping, apprehending, comprehension, and so on. What is being discussed here are the terms, the lexicon of philosophical thought. But the insight can be extended to the role of extended metaphor, models and analogies in structuring philosophical texts. One thinks immediately of the foundational model (e.g. in Descartes and Kant), the pervasiveness of spatial models in such notions as 'conceptual geography', 'logical space', and the spatial rhetoric of structuralist thought – of limits, discontinuities, thresholds and so on.

Nietzsche's claim can be followed up without passing any particular judgement on the argument that generated it. We can come to take an interest in the figurative structures of philosophical texts and wonder whether these might not be doing a lot more of the work than we had previously suspected. With Nietzsche we get something like the possibility of a psychoanalysis of texts, a left-handed reading.

In his book *The Garden of Epicurus*, Anatole France presents near the end a dialogue between two characters, Polyphilos and Aristos. The subject is the language of metaphysics. Polyphilos is in effect extending Nietzsche's position. What he claims is that all abstract concepts, the very substance of philosophy, are in fact dead metaphors, metaphors subject to such wear and tear that their sensible origins have been eliminated and forgotten. He suggests revitalizing the real meanings of abstract words, taking as an example: 'The spirit possesses God in proportion as it participates in the absolute.' The result (abbreviated) is this:

> The breath is seated on the shining one in the bushel of the part it takes in what is altogether loosed (or subtle). He whose breath is a sign of life, man, that is, will find a place in the divine fire, source and home of life . . .

He concludes from this recuperative experiment

> By an odd fate, the very metaphysicians who think to escape the world of appearance are constrained to live perpetually in allegory. A sorry lot of poets, they dim the colours of the ancient fables, and are themselves but authors of fables. They produce white mythology.[8]

So, according to Polyphilos, philosophy is permeated with metaphor without knowing it. In so far as philosophers do not realize that they are dealing with mere husks, they are living in a dream world of abstraction. They cannot acknowledge the metaphorical basis of abstraction, but neither can they escape it. The death of a metaphor is a purely negative affair, not the occasion for the birth of anything else. Put like this one might wonder whether the argument really works. For it does not follow from the fact that all abstract concepts have their historical roots in empirical ones that these roots are never escaped from. This would be an argument against butterflies being able to fly because of the winglessness of caterpillars. The possibility that a dead metaphor might be the positive ground of a live concept is one that we will take up with Ricoeur.

An obvious place to look for an account of extended metaphor is Stephen Pepper's book *World Hypotheses*. His basic claim is that all philosophy – he has traditional systematic philosophy most immediately in mind – is developed from one of a limited number of root metaphors. (The main four are Formism, Mechanism, Contextualism and Organicism.) So a crucial part of reading and understanding a philosophical theory would be realizing which root metaphor was being deployed. And on Pepper's view there is no rational basis for choice between the results generated from different world hypotheses. Now this might seem to endorse what we might almost call metaphorical reductionism. But it does not. For Pepper thinks of his root metaphors as providing what he calls the evidential source of the categories of a philosophical system. These categories form a secondary abstract sphere, with cognitive power. And this cognitive power can be measured by what he calls 'their capacity to acquire unrestricted structural corroboration'. He thinks of philosophical systems as 'world hypotheses', and while they are never directly refuted they are more or less fruitful in organizing our understanding of the world. The importance of this reference to corroboration is that a philosophical system has a basis for being evaluated which is independent of its metaphorical roots. Metaphor in philosophy on Pepper's view is productive of conceptual thinking which can then be judged by its fertility and explanatory power.

A similar position is taken up by Ricoeur in Chapter 8 of *The Rule of Metaphor*. In his detailed assessment of Nietzsche, Heidegger and Derrida, one claim stands out: that while there are intimate connections between what he calls 'poetic discourse' or 'metaphorical expression', on the one hand, and 'philosophical' or 'speculative' discourse on the other, these connections do not threaten the autonomy of philosophy. And Ricoeur tried to defend this claim against the Nietzschean tendencies we have outlined: 'It is important to recognize in principle the discontinuity that assures the autonomy of speculative discourse.' (p. 258) And he denies that philosophy 'simply reproduces the semantic workings of poetic discourse on the speculative plane'. His reasons are two-fold. Firstly, while he accepts that philosophical discourse has, as one of its conditions of possibility, 'the semantic dynamism of metaphorical expression' he says it is a mistake to suppose that conditions of possibility circumscribe the subsequent development of what they make possible. Indeed, he talks of philosophy as responding to 'the semantic possibilities of metaphor' by taking it up and articulating it in a new mode. This is very much the view we found in Pepper. Secondly, he thinks of metaphor – living metaphor, *metaphore vive* – as constantly returning to provide conceptual discourse – philosophy – with the occasion to 'think more'. It introduces 'the spark of imagination'. Creative imagination is nothing other than this demand (to 'think more') put to conceptual thought.

And here Ricoeur goes beyond Pepper. For not only does living metaphor make a philosophical system possible, it is also seen as providing the basis for the renewal and continuing life of reason by offering imaginative challenges.

Paul de Man, in his essay 'The epistemology of metaphor' initially offered philosophy two alternatives: 'It appears that philosophy either has to give up its constitutive claim to rigor in order to come to terms with the figurality of its language, or that it has to free itself from figuration altogether.' These options can be represented by Nietzsche and the purity thesis respectively. He went on, 'And if the latter is considered impossible, philosophy could at least learn to control figuration by keeping it, so to speak in its place, by delimiting the boundaries of its influence and thus restricting the epistemological damage that it may cause.'[9]

This last possibility captures Ricoeur's project quite well. Clearly, looking back at this third stage, the revenge of metaphor need not be destructive of philosophy (as it could be said to be in Nietzsche). It can simply be a massive reassertion of the positive constructive role of metaphor in philosophy, even while, as in Pepper and Ricoeur's cases, this role is limited.

But this return of metaphor to philosophy is not without its own problems. Might not this whole discourse on metaphor, for and against it, delimiting it, be itself predicated on the adequacy of the distinction between the metaphorical and the literal?

The metaphysics of metaphor

Heidegger's position is focused in the claim that 'the metaphorical exists only within the boundaries of metaphysics'.[10] This claim restricts the value of the concept of metaphor. For Heidegger understands metaphysics as a pervasive, but none the less delimitable feature of the history of philosophical thinking.

Metaphysics, for Heidegger, is philosophical thought alienated from the question of being. As such it includes all philosophy since Plato. For since the early Greek philosophers the original interrogative openness of being has been progressively and successively covered over by systems of categories, fundamental distinctions and oppositions which have become deaf to the basic questions and experiences to which they were the response. Heidegger, like Nietzsche (whom he none the less criticizes), sees metaphysics as a finite and determinate set of options. What he attempts in his later writings is not to go beyond metaphysics, but to do something different. As we shall see this requires a new relation to language.

But one's first reaction to Heidegger's later writing is that it is *packed* with metaphor. Heidegger takes issue with this. He insists on a number of occasions that we should not understand his sentences metaphorically. In his *Letter on Humanism* he remarks that 'language is the House of Being'. This he says is not to be taken metaphorically. And the caution does not only apply to his own writings. When Hölderlin, in his poem *Bread and Wine*, uses the expression 'words like flowers' and talks of language as the 'flower of the mouth' we should not interpret this as metaphor.[11] Moreover, in the very passage from which our original quotation (about metaphor and metaphysics) came, Heidegger tells us that when he says of *seeing* and *hearing* that they are ways of *thinking*, it is not, again, meant metaphorically. And yet it is equally clearly not meant literally. What he is claiming is that the very distinction between metaphorical and literal is one that makes sense only within a metaphysical framework.

For Heidegger, the judgement that the remark about seeing, hearing and thinking is metaphorical would rest on the assignment of seeing and hearing to the *sensory* level and thinking to the intelligible or *non-sensory*. A remark that conjoined these two levels could only be metaphysical. Heidegger attributes the sensory/non-sensory distinction to metaphysics, and concludes that 'the metaphorical exists only within the boundaries of the metaphysical'. So when Wittgenstein[12] and Hanson[13] argue that there are no pure sounds, that we hear motorbikes not 'sounds', they are attacking not just the distinction between the sensory and the non-sensory, but metaphysics itself.

One problem with the argument is that it draws a general conclusion about metaphor in general from a *particular feature* of the example chosen, the fact that the distinction between the sensible and the non-sensible is at work in it. But it is certainly not generally true (and Ricoeur would concur with this criticism) that metaphor makes use of this particular opposition. If I say 'my house is my cocoon' I am probably just comparing it to a cocoon in respect of its warmth and safety. The distinction between the sensible and the non-sensible does not seem to enter, unless we treat the idea of a detachable attribute (e.g. warmth, safety) on which metaphor certainly does seem to rest, as somehow implicated in the sensory/non-sensory distinction. Nietzsche at one stage did hold this view, but did Heidegger? And if he did, why risk a failure of generalizability discussing a case in which the sensory/non-sensory distinction is more directly at work?

One possible way out of this problem is to suppose that Heidegger is proposing a more restricted thesis: that the predicate 'metaphor' plays a regulating role within metaphysics, policing the boundaries between different types of being, between different categories, by labelling all trans-categorial utterances 'metaphorical', so ensuring that they do not threaten metaphysical discourse, because they are not taken seriously. On this interpretation, however, it would be *philosophical* metaphor that would have been shown to be intimately connected to metaphysics, and the argument verges on mere explication of that phrase.

But Heidegger doesn't want this restriction. Recall the reference to Hölderlin, and indeed Heidegger's own more meditative writing. Heidegger objects to some or all of this being thought metaphorical. Returning to our original argument, Heidegger says that the collapse of 'metaphor' has a decisive effect in particular on the way in which we represent the being of language.

'Language', he says, not *'philosophical* language'. And yet he does talk about *representing* the *being* of language. Heidegger wants to generalize his criticism of the concept of metaphor to its application to language as a whole, because he thinks – and here I am glossing over many problems – that an authentic relationship to language is one in which language is never an object, never subjected to a disciplined ordering of predicates and their proper application, but is rather a gift that opens a world to us, and to which there is in a sense no outside. At this point I could have easily said 'Language is the house of Being', as Heidegger does in *Letter on Humanism*. But does not this sentence only explain away metaphor by using metaphor? Heidegger insists again he is not writing metaphorically. Let us listen to what his translator has him say: 'The talk about the house of Being is no transfer of the image 'house' to Being. But one day, we will, by thinking the essence of Being in an appropriate(ing) way . . . more readily be able to think what 'house' and 'to dwell' are.'[14]

Now one *could* construe this sentence as a complex metaphor, perhaps a two-way metaphor, the direction switching back and forth. But before doing this we ought to notice something this sentence shares with the Hölderlin phrase 'words, like flowers', that it is not just an ordinary sentence, however complex. It is about *language*. And it aims to establish a certain relationship between language and being.

And if we have understood Heidegger aright, this relationship is one which squeezes out just such notions as metaphor. So as I read it: when we unpack this sentence we discover that *it itself* rejects metaphor.

There is a whole additional complexity which I will mention but not explore. Metaphor is classically based on the distinction between those predicates which belong to a certain subject and those that do not belong. There is some sense in which the concept of metaphor is involved in the question of 'home' or what it is to say that things 'belong' somewhere. (Was Wittgenstein drawing on such a notion when he talked about philosophical problems arising when 'language goes on holiday'?)

For Heidegger, the problematic of *dwelling* goes back to the account of authenticity he gave in *Being and Time*. We can be furthest away from ourselves when we seem closest; *dwelling* is not merely being *in* a world (in the everyday sense of spatial containedness). Later (*On the Way to Language*) he tells us that the important thing in thinking is not to get anywhere (else) but to get to where one is already, that is, to transform one's being, and in particular one's relation to language.

This project of transforming language is taken up by Derrida as the project of a new form of writing, which could be called 'parametaphysical'[15] And it is to this project that I now turn.

Derrida and metaphor

As with Heidegger, Derrida's account of metaphor is one that informs and is informed by a theory and practice of writing. The main repositories of his views are his essays 'White mythology'(1971) and 'The *retrait* of metaphor' (1978).[16] To understand what Derrida says about metaphor, and how he takes up or transforms Heidegger's position, there is no substitute for at least a minimal summary of his general understanding of language.

What is distinctive about Derrida's position is his understanding of language not via some relation to being (as in Heidegger) but as a play of differences. This play is more or less ordered in particular texts, but fundamentally uncontrollable. The idea of a play of differences is the consequence of Derrida's radicalization of Saussure's account of a language as a system of phonological and semantic differences. Meaning is no longer thought of as dependent on reference, but on the differences that separate and distinguish words and their meanings.

Derrida's radicalization consisted of rejecting as residual metaphysics this distinction between phonology and semantics, or words and meanings. The distinction between these two is itself 'in play'. So there is, if you like, horizontal and vertical play at the same time.

This account has important consequences for our understanding of metaphor. For the notion of metaphor presupposes a level of semantic stability that Derrida has long since left behind. To say that metaphor determined philosophy would be misleading. It is rather that a certain understanding of philosophy is unceasingly threatened by the vertical play between sound and meaning, as well as between sounds and between meanings. When Derrida titles his second essay on metaphor 'The *retrait* of metaphor', he means among other things that with the disappearance of the idea of the literal, so the concept of metaphor also withdraws from the scene. But as we shall see this word withdrawal (*retrait*) has many other senses that Derrida does not hesitate to exploit.

I shall now explore Derrida's views about the status of the philosophy/metaphor relationship, a relationship of considerable subtlety, through three points of comparison with Heidegger.

First, Derrida claims we have to 'borrow from metaphor' in order to talk about it. The argument goes something like this. Let us accept, with Heidegger, that metaphor is a metaphysical concept, that, for example, the metaphorical/literal distinction relies on some notion of the proper meaning of words, and on the distinction between the sensible and the non-sensible or intelligible. Derrida also believes that it is impossible in principle to just step outside of metaphysics. One cannot do without the tools of metaphysics when deconstructing it. Deconstruction works from within, or on the boundaries of the metaphysical, not from a privileged point outside. It would follow that there is no possibility of abandoning or eliminating metaphor precisely because of its link to metaphysics.

So while Derrida will also reconstruct Heidegger's claims about the non-metaphorical status of his claims, Derrida himself recognizes that a new kind of philosophical writing requires strategic self-transformation rather than a leap outside.

For our second point of comparison with Heidegger I focus on Derrida's insistence that Heidegger's linking of metaphor to metaphysics via the sensible/non-sensible distinction is too limited. Much of the point of Derrida's 'White mythology' is to show that the concept of metaphor is constituted not by a single opposition at all, but by a whole discourse (one is tempted to say metaphorical discourse) on metaphor – the whole range of concepts and associations by which metaphor is comprehended and given a place: wear and tear (abstract concepts are just worn out metaphors), life and death (living and dead metaphors), transportation, transference, transposition, use/usage/usury, home, proper place, and so on.

What Derrida is trying to do is to displace and reduce any reduction of metaphor to one opposition, and to locate the concept of metaphor itself within a play of differences.

Thus at the beginning of 'The *retrait* of metaphor' we are engulfed by an extended play with the association between metaphor and transportation:'We are in a certain way – metaphorically of course, and as concerns the mode of habitation – the content and the tenor of this vehicle: passengers, comprehended and displaced by metaphor'.[17] As with Heidegger there is the suggestion that we are inside language. But instead of this *inside* being a dwelling, we seem this time to be always on the move. To be invaded by metaphor is to be invaded by semantic play, by instability. Where Heidegger offers hard-won comfort at the end of the day, Derrida offers permanent displacement, dislocation.

And Derrida does not stop at discursively distributing the concept of metaphor. He also examines and elaborates on two of the families of words with which Heidegger himself organizes his own account of metaphor and language (those connected with *Ziehen* and *Reissen*).

This takes us to the third point of comparison between Derrida and Heidegger. I mean here Derrida's reconstruction of Heidegger's account of the concept of metaphor through the term withdrawal (*retrait*). The second half of 'The *retrait* of metaphor' is a reading of Heidegger. Derrida explains why he chose the word *retrait*.[18] His project is a reading of Heidegger on metaphor. He seems to understand a reading as a kind of capture of one text by another. The most efficient way of doing that seems to be to try and relate it, in multiple ways to a key term – in this case *retrait*, which functions as a kind of drag-net through Heidegger's texts. He uses it the way one might try to harvest the weed from a pond by dragging a net, or a coil of barbed wire through it. The barbs here are the multiplicity of meanings and associations of the word *retrait*. He writes 'I presumed the word *retrait* . . . to be the most proper to capture the greatest quantity of energy and information in the Heideggerian text.' What does he do with Heidegger?

Beginning from Heidegger's understanding of metaphysics as a bracketing, *epoché* or withdrawal of the history of being, Derrida discovers an intimacy between metaphysics and metaphor that we have so far not considered. He suggests that

> the whole of this aforesaid history of Western metaphysics would be a vast structural process where the *epoché* of Being withholding itself in withdrawal, would take, or rather would present an (interlaced) series of guises, of turns, of modes, that is to say, of figures or of tropical aspects which we would be tempted to describe with the aid of rhetorical conceptuality.[19]

We are left with a strange folded, involuted or as he puts it 'invaginated' structure: 'Metaphysics would not only be the enclosure in which the concept of metaphor ... would be produced and enclosed ... it would itself be in a tropical (metaphorical) position with regard to Being and the thought of Being'.[20] Derrida pushes this paradox to the extreme. If we suppose that the metaphorical/literal distinction has its proper application to beings (things, worldly relations) we cannot *literally* talk of the withdrawal of being, or the relationship of metaphysics to it, as metaphorical.

What are we to make of this? I think Derrida's aim here is not just to demonstrate how clever one can be in manipulating the concept of metaphor, but first to show that the choice is not between the metaphysical status of metaphor and the metaphorical status of metaphysics, but rather an appreciation of the complex structure that encloses them both, and second to claim that the movement of withdrawal by which metaphysics is constituted cannot be completely subsumed under the term metaphor. It is, if you like, an original difference, a differentiation and a deferment.

Derrida's advance on Heidegger can be described like this: while Heidegger may have released us from a naive acceptance of the metaphor/literal distinction he ends up giving language a new sacredness, posing too much as the 'personal secretary of Being'.[21] Derrida shows that the play of signifiers never ends, and affirms it.

Conclusion

The discussion here of the involvement of philosophy with metaphor is guided by an interest in philosophical method. Each of the positions considered has consequences for writing and reading philosophy. On the purity thesis, reading would typically involve an eliminative

40

translation of figures. On Nietzsche's position it would be an attempt to decode the figural structures of a text. On Ricoeur's position, reading would mark the division between the poetic and the philosophical. And much the same could be said in each case for writing. If we are concerned with how we might read and write philosophy, and if this chapter maps out a kind of itinerary of possibilities, then what are we to make of its destination? What consequences for reading and writing would follow from, say, the Derrida/Heidegger accounts of metaphor? I claim not to have demonstrated the necessity of this route but only its possibility. And one might well respond to it in the light of the philosophical approaches it opens up.

One feature seems to call for immediate attention. For Derrida the distinction between reading and writing is a difficult one to make. Even if we do not centre our whole account around one concept like deconstruction, it is still true that Derrida's philosophical method is unashamedly second order. The core of everything he has written is a commentary on, reconstruction, analysis, dislocation of . . . another text – not always but often a philosophical text. So while we might say that the Derridean texts we have mentioned here are both *on* metaphor, in fact they dealt with philosophical texts *about* metaphor. I say *unashamedly* second order; there are for Derrida no philosophical problems outside textual elaboration, so it might be that the second order would be the first, or original order. The germs may appear in the form of reflection on, or talk about real-life situations, but we only get philosophy when these are textually elaborated and articulated.

There is no *a priori* demand that philosophy concern itself with philosophical texts. A newspaper article might supply just as suitable material. But again, we confirm the model: for Derrida, writing is in the end 'reading', and reading writing.

How does metaphor come into this? Derrida's philosophical methods can be characterized as a self-conscious, transformative rewriting of another text, one that draws out the figurative 'structure' of this text(s) not with the intention of bringing out thereby its latent meaning, but so as to articulate the semantic strategies and economies of a text. What one might call a concern with the metaphorical infrastructure of a text is qualified by Derrida in two ways; these qualifications constitute his self-consciousness.

First, he denies the implicit reference to the proper literal meaning that this would imply. Rather we are offered an economy of differences, intermeshed webs of terms, a complex play of differences.

Second, this whole scene is itself 'made possible' by the absence of any presence, fullness of meaning, being – which he calls withdrawal. So we have a kind of transcendental theory of textuality.

Philosophy finds its limits here not in a restriction of its outer scope, but in a necessary entanglement with that from which it thinks it must free itself. Such 'entanglement' is the very condition of its textual articulation: *mere* 'metaphor' no longer.

Should we be attracted by this approach or is Derrida just a star performer whom one can admire or revile but not learn from? Does Derrida offer a publicly available method?

The usual objection to Derrida – and its basis would seem amply confirmed by 'The *retrait* of metaphor' – is that his orientation to texts is a new kind of idealism, one that takes the form of 'a precious little pedagogy' (as Foucault put it). And if the idealists did not change the world, at least in interpreting it they related to it minimally. Derrida only interprets texts.

The fastest answer to this is to consider the role of texts – philosophical, scientific, legal – in legitimation of established orders of things. One of the consequences of a deconstruction of such texts is something like delegitimation,[22] which may well have effects on the 'world'.

The positive value of Derrida's approach is that it does at least potentially allow us to re-read the history of philosophy with an attention to detail that some of the alternative versions would not require or allow. While Derrida's readings are selectively directed to certain features of texts, they amplify and elaborate them. Deconstruction is not reductionistic in any simple way, it is a critique that operates on the blind side of philosophical practice.

Notes

1 Cf. Gadamer's *Philosophical Hermeneutics* (Berkeley and Los Angeles: University of California Press, 1976), p. 3.
2 There have been conferences, essays, books, and certainly everywhere interest. To name just three books: Ricoeur's *The Rule of Metaphor* (London: Routledge, 1978), Ortony's collection *Metaphor and Thought* (Cambridge: Cambridge University Press, 1979) and Sheldon Sacks' Critical Inquiry collection *On Metaphor* (Chicago: University of Chicago Press, 1979).
3 Gilbert Ryle, *The Concept of Mind* (London: Hutchinson, 1949).
4 *Enquiry Concerning Human Understanding* (London: Dent, [1690] 1961), Book 3, Ch. 9.
5 *Thinking to Some Purpose* (Harmondsworth: Penguin, 1939), p. 113.
6 This is discussed by Derrida in his 'White Mythology', in *Margins of Philosophy* [1972] (Chicago: University of Chicago Press, 1982).

7 From 'Truth and Falsity in their Ultra-Moral sense' [1873], in N. Languilli (ed.), *The Existentialist Tradition* (New York: Anchor, 1971) p. 80.

8 See Anatole France, *The Garden of Epicurus*, trans. Alfred Allinson (New York: Dodd Mead, [1900] 1923). This last phrase – in the original, 'mythologie blanche' – is of course the title Derrida gives to his own first essay on metaphor (see note 6).

9 'The epistemology of Metaphor', in *On Metaphor*, p. 11.

10 *Der Satz vom Grund* [1956] (Pfullingen: Neske, 1971).

11 'On the way to language', in *On the Way to Language* [1959] (New York: Harper & Row, 1971), p. 100.

12 *Philosophical Investigations* (Oxford: Blackwell, 1953).

13 *Patterns of Discovery* (Cambridge: Cambridge University Press, 1958).

14 *Letter on Humanism* [1947], in *Basic Writings*, ed. D. F. Krell (New York: Harper & Row, 1977) pp. 236–7.

15 *Oxford English Dictionary* (OED): *para-* is defined as a Greek preposition. It had the sense of 'by the side of, besides' whence 'alongside of, by, past, beyond, etc.' In composition it had the same senses, with such cognate adverb ones as 'to one side, amiss, faulty, irregular, disordered, improper, wrong'.

16 'The *retrait* of metaphor', *Enclitic*, vol II, no. 2, fall 1978.

17 ibid., p. 6.

18 ibid., pp. 18–19.

19 ibid., p. 20. Compare Hayden White's *Metahistory* (Baltimore: Johns Hopkins, 1973).

20 'The *retrait* of metaphor', pp. 20–21.

21 I owe this phrase to David Krell.

22 See my 'An introduction to Derrida', in R. Edgley and R. Osborne (eds), *Radical Philosophy Reader*, (London: Verso, 1985), pp. 14–42.

Further reading

Andrew Ortony's collection *Metaphor and Thought* (Cambridge, 1979) and Sheldon Sacks's collection *On Metaphor* contain between them an excellent core of papers from both an analytical point of view and from within literary theory. Ortony includes papers by Max Black, L. J. Cohen and John Searle, while Sacks has Donald Davidson's 'What Metaphors Mean' and shorter contributions from Quine and Goodman. Ortony's exceptionally rich collection includes a contribution from Kuhn on 'Metaphor in Science', while Sacks has important papers by de Man and Ricoeur.

Derrida's two papers on metaphor, 'White mythology' [1972] and 'The *retrait* of metaphor' [1978] (in *Margins of Philosophy* [Chicago: University of Chicago Press, 1982]) constitute something of a debate with Ricoeur's *The Rule of Metaphor* (London: Routledge, [1975] 1978) especially Chapter 8, 'Metaphor and Philosophical Discourse'. One would have to add to this Heidegger's *On the Way to Language* [1959] (Harper & Row, 1971) and 'Letter on Humanism' (in *Basic Writings*, ed. David Krell [Harper & Row, 1977]). Both Ricoeur and Derrida take for granted the problematizing of metaphor that Heidegger engages in.

3

Deconstruction and criticism

What I attempt in this chapter, with all the dangers that are inevitably involved, is to present 'deconstruction', as practised largely by Derrida, as a critical philosophical method, one that makes a distinct advance on other such methods, and one worthy of general adoption. I shall try to explain what makes it distinctive, why it has been less than favourably received, and what place it could have in a philosophical repertoire.

The dangers I mentioned concern my apparently uncritical appeal to 'philosophy' as if it were not itself put in question by 'deconstruction'. And there is also the danger of blunting the edge of deconstruction by presenting it as a useful addition to our repertoire of philosophical techniques. But if there are errors, it is not clear who or what is at risk. Surely it could not be a proper grasp of deconstruction that is threatened? Anyway we may learn more by making errors and correcting them than by never making them in the first place.

I will argue that deconstruction performs on philosophy itself an operation which philosophy normally applies to the world, to our experience of it, or to our thoughts about it. But I am taking for granted here a certain view of the nature and function of philosophy that I ought perhaps to state and briefly defend. Philosophers do all sorts of things, explain, analyse, argue, construct, criticize, etc. but the operation that seems quite central is defamiliarization, or distancing onself from the taken-for-granted. When a philosopher asks how something is possible, it is a question that points forward to an answer, or attempts to provide an answer, one that declares an estranged distance from the given, the everyday. Clearly philosophy is not entirely alone in this. Poetry, science (in certain of its moments) and religion also have this defamiliarizing power, not to mention dreams, drugs, foreign travel and science fiction. One has to make reference to the particular positive procedures employed, such as rational explanation unadulterated by faith or experimentation, to distinguish the specifically philosophical

44

form of defamiliarization. On this account, then, philosophy is a mode of defamiliarization that bears within itself as an ideal the possibility of rationally organizing our belief about the world. It takes as its subject matter not just common-sense beliefs but also those of science and religion and where it clashes with beliefs already rationally organized, we talk of philosophy's defamiliarizing action as 'criticism'.

As a point of reference, perhaps I should say that I am aligning myself with what Rorty calls, perhaps ill-advisedly, the edifying philosophers rather than systematic philosophy. Edifying philosophy shows us that things need not be the way they seem to be; systematic philosophy tries to show us how things are and must be. A brief rationale for privileging the edifying conception over the systematic one, as we have done in introducing the idea of defamiliarization, might be that the systematic or constructive movement in philosophy always presupposes an original 'break', or distancing from the given. Its mistake is to treat this merely as the opportunity for reconstruction, rather than permanently clearing a space. Systematic philosophy mistakenly imitates the procedures of science. The proof of this is the lack of progress in philosophy. The best that can be said about its history is that certain of its techniques get more and more subtle and refined, but philosophical results – ones that stand the test of time – are in short supply.

There is a limit to the rational defensibility of the claim that philosophy is fundamentally edifying or defamiliarizing. I would like to think it is this that sustains it, and that funds its perpetual self-renewal. But I am not really out to demonstrate this claim here so much as to make it explicit. For it allows me to offer a brief, perhaps too simple, formula for what is involved in deconstruction. Deconstruction reflexively applies to philosophy itself the defamiliarizing operation philosophy usually reserves for outer application. The kinds of responses this will arouse can already be anticipated. Deconstruction is negative, destructive, will mean the end of philosophy; it is subversive of philosophical confidence, threatens philosophical vigour; it is sterile and unproductive, and so on. Equally it could be said to involve a kind of contradiction, making use of standards (e.g. rational accountability) which it will surely put in question. Finally it could be regarded as poor form, or bad strategy. Philosophy has enemies enough; we should not feed the enemy within.

What form does this reflexive operation take? Deconstruction is usually described by its proponents as a way or method of reading. (It has been developed as a way of reading literary texts, especially at Yale; I want here to restrict my attention to its philosophical applications.) But what then distinguishes it from other forms of philosophical criticism? How unusual is it in fact for philosophy to be self-critical in the sense of involving the critical reading of other philosophical texts? What more is involved in deconstruction? The key to the specific reflexivity of a deconstructive reading is that the features of a philosophical text that it picks on are not the logical inconsistencies, the weak arguments, the unlikely premises (although these might indeed serve pleasantly to wash down the critical meal) but rather the features which are philosophically most respectable, the features that make the text a philosophical text ... Philosophical deconstruction concerns itself with what is philosophical in a text not what fails to meet some philosophical standard or other. That is why I said that deconstruction is the application to philosophy of the operation of defamiliarization. For there is a strong sense in which, in each individual text Derrida deals with, it is the possibility of philosophy itself that is at stake, not simply the adequacy of a particular text. The kinds of moves he makes would apply to any text, and so the force of a particular deconstruction can easily be generalized.

It is something of a slogan (rather than the clear expression of a fundamental insight) to say that all philosophy is writing. And there are all sorts of claims that one might think were being made that are not, so it would be as well to begin by clarifying this statement. Although deconstruction has, in the hands of Derrida, in fact been a heavily inter-textual affair, concerning itself not so much with issues as with the particular texts of other writers and philosophers, the aim is not, for example, to exclude oral discussion from the status of philosophy. Writing has here something of a philosophical rather than a purely empirical sense to it. To say that all philosophy is writing is, minimally, to say that it is never the transparent expression of thought. It is always embodied in systems of signs which have an inalienably material character, both as phonic or graphic substance (sound or ink ...) and in being composed of signs that have already been used in other contexts. Philosophical language does not come from heaven; the dream of a final purification (of the literary, everyday, past philosophical usage) is just that – a dream. And to all this, as a final gloss on 'philosophy as writing', one could add that philosophy is always textual. By this is meant that the primary unit of meaning is not the word, nor the sentence, but a collection of sentences, a text, animated by the structure of the trace, by which any particular text's boundaries are necessarily compromised by its interlacings and resonances with other texts.

What status do these claims have? Something of their force comes from the way they combine uncontentious empirical claims that philosophy always takes place in complexly articulated language, and that language always has a material side to it, with claims about the theoretical consequences that flow from these facts, such as 'no transparent expression of thought'. The status of *this* claim is as difficult to assess as general claims about translatability. Indeed the claim that complete translation is impossible within natural languages would seem both to follow from the no transparency principle, and to share its problematic status.

What is thought to follow from these various claims is something like this: that the capacity of philosophy to make claims the significance of which transcends the particularity of the language in which they are embodied is compromised by the material of any natural language. The ideal of such transcendence as is possessed by mathematics or logic is just not available for philosophy within a natural language. But this is only a bare abstract fact about language. More important are the ways in which the philosophical use of language does indeed seem to exhibit something like a legacy, transmitted from the original Greek thought to the present day. From the point of view of the practising philosopher, and discounting reservations about individual examples, the classical oppositions between nature/culture, fact/value, ideal/material, essential/accidental, etc. are the life-blood of philosophical argument. But from an external point of view, they can seem to constitute for philosophy a largely unargued taken-for-granted framework in which the challenging of any one particular opposition, for example, fact/value or analytic/synthetic, can have devastating consequences. Such oppositions it is true, are more usually used, gainfully employed in reasoning, than argued for. And it is a characteristic of the efficient use of a tool that one does not at the time question its legitimacy. In this case the very questioning process would itself be hard put to avoid taking other philosophical distinctions for granted. Derrida's reading of particular philosophical texts is such as to bring out structures and strategies constitutive of philosophy in general, but it would be mistaken to suppose that all he was interested in is deconstructing hard-working main-line oppositions. He is a master at exposing and, indeed, subverting what we could call the latent textuality of typical philosophical texts. While it is perfectly clear that most decently constructed philosophical writings have something like a rational organization in which one can isolate premisses, arguments and conclusions without too great a strain on the intellect, there is another level at which one can discuss the organization of a philosophical text, the level of its unconscious textuality. This rests on a view about, indeed perhaps even what can look like a *theory* of philosophy, one Derrida more or less shares with Heidegger, and one which typically arouses a peculiar hostility when made explicit. I will try to state this in as clear a way as possible at the risk of oversimplification.

We have already met the claim that philosophy is writing, with the various corollaries attached to it. What we need to add now is the claim that it is a considerable part of the philosophical project to escape from its status as writing, to transcend the particularity of its physical form, the actual language it employs. It would like the language it uses to be a transparent vehicle of meaning and truth. It always appeals to a ground/source/origin/standard of meaning that would escape the vagaries of writing. It claims and seeks independence from its medium or vehicle of expression. Yet this is impossible. And the attempt to realize it on any particular occasion is marked by a series of displacements, substitutions, of one term for another within a text that defer the point at which this extralinguistic value is deemed to have been grasped. Such a series of displacements exhibits what Derrida calls the structure of supplementarity, in which something apparently complete is added to, to make up for what it is subsequently seen to have lacked. A philosophical text chases what Derrida calls *presence* – self-sufficient and accessible points of reference, values, unequivocal terms, etc. and it does so interminably and (necessarily) without success. A deconstructive reading of a particular philosophical text would bring out these chains of substitution, would unravel the latent itinerary, the hidden agenda.

Deconstruction is based, if you like, on a radical incompleteness thesis. Unlike Descartes, Kant, Hegel, Husserl, Carnap . . . to name but a few, who proposed radical new ways of achieving the firm results that philosophy had so conspicuously failed to produce, ways that usually involved making philosophy into a 'science', deconstruction offers something like an account of why such projects could never be successful. One is tempted to draw parallels with mathematical proofs of the impossibility of proving certain theorems. The parallel is instructive, however, in the differences it brings to light.

I said that deconstruction rests on a *theory* of philosophy. Deconstruction cannot be *reduced* to a 'theory' of philosophy, but it is an analytical theory of the relationship between certain ideals (e.g. the transparent articulation of the structure of knowledge, the idea of the good . . .) and the mode of their attempted realization (i.e. writing). Philosophy – sometimes Heidegger and Derrida will speak of philosophy and metaphysics more or less co-terminously – is the name traditionally, and even today, given to that project. At a certain point, as I have suggested, there is an appeal to a philosophy of language, broadly post-Saussurean in outline, the credentials of which rest on the appeal of its anti-essentialist theory of meaning, on its fertility in reading literary as well as philosophical texts, and on its ability to accommodate if not elaborate those phenomena on which other theories of language might focus. We do not get from Derrida a theory of speech acts,[1] but we do get a deconstruction of the ideas of intention and context essential to it.

At this point I would like briefly to allude to some of the critical readings Derrida has made of other philosophers, with a view to illuminating the nature of deconstruction. But for those who would prefer an explicit definition rather than illustrations, Derrida offers an account of the general strategy of deconstruction (in *Positions*). It involves – and here I am analytically reconstructing his account – three stages: (1) the identification within a text of a constitutive hierarchical opposition, in which one term is systematically privileged; (2) the overturning of this opposition, for example by demonstrating interdependence, or suggesting the reverse privilege; (3) the introduction into the text of a new term which is undecidable in terms of the old opposition. This may indeed just be one of the original terms recycled with a different scope.

This is somewhat schematic. To give more idea of the diversity of deconstructive strategies I will briefly discuss Derrida's treatments of three other philosophers – Husserl, Rousseau and Austin.

Derrida on Husserl

Husserl tried to provide, in his *Logical Investigations*, a grounding in ideal acts of consciousness for the most basic concepts of logic, and indeed theoretical discourse in general. The word *Logical* in the title can mislead us. He is in fact offering what could be called an analytical theory of rational discourse in general ('science') in which the most basic concepts of any rational discipline would be given a grounding in intuitive self-evidence.

Husserl thought it not only possible but philosophically vital to preserve a reference to meaning-constituting acts of consciousness, while avoiding the philosophically destructive charge of psychologism brought against his earlier work by Frege. He insisted that he was concerned only with ideal acts, not with the particular empirical psychological acts individual people might perform. He was convinced that some such reference to a pre-linguistic layer of meaning was essential to distinguish, for instance, a merely formulaically presented truth $(2 + 2 = 4)$ in which the symbols involved are employed without any grasp of their significance (e.g. by a machine or as a cliché) and the same sentence uttered thoughtfully, and with a grasp of the meaning of the symbols involved. The distinction between empty and fulfilled meaning would apply to all languages, not just mathematical formulae.

And while he devotes the first volume to *Prolegomena to Pure Logic*, in which he argues for the need for a pure logic, and against any empirically psychologistic understanding of it, the second volume, the *Investigations* proper, begins with a discussion quite as pertinent to language in general as logic in any narrow sense, of *Expression and Meaning* and it is on this investigation that Derrida focuses his interest in *Speech and Phenomena*. Whatever may or may not be fundamental to logic, what is fundamental to Husserl's account of it is his distinction between two kinds of signs, or two functions of signs, indication (*Anzeichen*) and expression (*Ausdruck*).

Basically indications, from the point of view of meaning, are empty. They are arbitrarily connected by association to something else (like the knot in a handkerchief). Expressions, on the other hand contain meaning in themselves. Since, for Husserl, language proper consists of expression, the distinction between indication and expression is vital. Clearly, to carry it through, some account of how expressive signs do indeed bear meaning within themselves is needed. For Husserl, actual public speech is an impure mixture of indication and expression. He reserves pure cases of expression (and hence of language) for the purity of 'solitary mental life' where externality and hence indication are excluded. Here one can silently infuse signs with meaning by conscious intentional acts.

Husserl's appeal is to what Derrida calls the purity of self-presence. And Derrida's deconstructive reading consists of three stages. First, he denies the purity of Husserl's ideal meanings, by insisting that ideality is (and then only incompletely) produced by repetition. This move we could think of as a kind of nominalism. Second, Husserl supposes that expression in inner monologue takes place in the imagination. But, as Derrida points out, imagination too is possible only by repetitions of past experiences, associations, etc. And finally, Husserl's account of the purity of self-presence is undermined by his own account of the role of past and future in constituting the present.

For all these reasons, the basis of the expression/indication distinction is seen to evaporate. Expression is not merely empirically but essentially interwoven with indication and the attempt to eliminate indication must fail. If indication cannot be eliminated, then the ideal of self-presence is radically undermined. If, as Derrida claims, phenomenology as a whole rests on establishing a human realm of self-presence free from external indication, then phenomenology too is being challenged.[2]

Derrida on Rousseau

Rousseau expresses a considerable hostility to writing, as opposed to speech. On his most insistent account, writing is a mere supplement to speech. Speech is living, personal, natural . . . while writing is merely an adjunct or accessory to speech, a way of standing in for speech when this could not be had. This view of writing is quite traditional. And yet Rousseau's text subverts itself when we find for instance that Rousseau condemns writing as unnatural (which suggests a position different from mere derivativeness) and then goes on to say how important it is for him to be a writer, for otherwise people might suppose him to actually be as boring and uninteresting a person as he often is in the flesh. The unnaturalness of writing is a theme echoed by Saussure, who as a first move in the construction of a general theory of language (semiology) excludes writing as secondary, derivative, the mere sign of a sign, and yet, contradictorily, producing monstrous interferences with living spoken language.

Rousseau's denunciation of writing as unnatural, and his return to embrace it to supplement his own deficient social presence is claimed by Derrida to illustrate a general structure of supplementarity, one that typically structures philosophical texts. What is deemed natural or complete, or primitive, or brute, is seen to need completion, adding on to, supplementing, by that which it has previously treated as impure, external, secondary, derived ... or in this case 'unnatural'.

Derrida demonstrates brilliantly how this same structure is repeated in Rousseau's discussion of his own dangerous and unnatural vice – masturbation – which is both a substitute for normal sexuality, second best, and yet in the complete (albeit fantasied) power one has to seduce any woman it can even come to seem superior. And if one thinks of real loving affection as involving a considerable degree of imagination and projection, it is possible to come to see normal sexuality as an impure example of the pure form of masturbation.

Rousseau's case is particularly interesting for understanding deconstruction because it is he himself who in a sense initiates the deconstruction of the value of the natural, and Derrida's role here is just to point it out, consolidate it, and draw the moral.[3]

Derrida on Austin

After a cult following in Oxford in the 1950s, the patient, idiosyncratically textual approach of the philosopher J. L. Austin suffered from a general backlash against the irrelevance of a purely linguistic philosophy. But his work has lived on in the speech-act theory actively promulgated by John Searle,[4] and he has even, ironically, been recently elevated to the rank of a proto-deconstructor by Christopher Norris.[5]

Austin begins *How to Do Things with Words* (1962) with a distinction that must seem to most of his readers both sensible and innocuous, that between serious and non-serious utterances. Non-serious utterances, which include those made on stage, those made jokingly, those that occur in reported speech, in novels, etc. are put to one side because they are deemed parasitical on the serious, standard form, in which people speak deliberately, and mean what they say in an ordinary way. The idea is that we can only intelligibly utter words on stage, for example, if it would make sense to utter them in ordinary discourse.

In his paper 'Signature event context'[6] Derrida contests among other things the innocence of this distinction. In his view, the relation of one-way parasitical dependence itself depends on the idea of the self-contained intelligibility of the idea of 'intention', the fully self-present understanding of what one is doing in serious utterances. But instead of suggesting, as some analytical philosophers have done, that a reference to convention is needed, or a reference to a second order intention to be understood, Derrida argues for the dependence of the intention that constitutes seriousness on what is non-intentional, on, for example, the possibility of making sense of the utterance in such non-intentional cases as an inscription, in a book where the author and context may be absent or unknown. There is a parallel with the usual reference to convention, but it is as it were a nominalistic version that makes no reference to rules. Derrida's claim can perhaps be put like this (and I put it here in what may turn out to be a misleading way): it is a condition for the expressing of an intention that it fasten itself to some form of words, which in each case derives its capacity to capture such an intention from the fact of being repeated and repeatable in other contexts – not excluding, and precisely including, non-serious ones. Derrida is claiming that the possible instantiations of a form of words are not consequences of its meaning, but constitutive of that meaning. If so, the distinction between the serious and the non-serious, in which the latter is made derivative from the former, disguises a dependence relation between any particular expression (serious/non-serious) and other serious and non-serious embodiments.

It might be said that there is a confusion between something like force and meaning, and that while Derrida is right to say that the meaning of an utterance is dependent on its infinite iterability, its force could not be dependent on cases in which that force (e.g. seriousness) was missing, so that, in Austin's language, what might just be true of locutionary acts is not true for illocutionary acts. However, the basis of Derrida's move seems clear enough, and it is one that, in a general way, has been followed by all those who deny a discrete essentialism of meanings. It is to deny that anything – even 'intention' – can dissolve the fact that meaning has its basis in systematic differences, both between the physical shapes and sounds of words and between the different contexts of their use. A crossroads need be no more than the point at which two roads cross; there need be no independently existing point at which they intersect. Meaning would be a consequence of differentiation, not its condition.

Are we then to conclude that philosophy is a vain pursuit? If deconstruction rests on an analytic account of the structure of the philosophical project *as commonly understood* is there not scope for a philosophy that would escape deconstruction? Derrida himself gestures towards something as yet nameless, which would be a new kind of writing, one that plays on and around the boundaries of philosophy, a kind of liminology. And the difficulty of classifying his work, and coming to terms with, say, the undecidable terms he introduces, would suggest that he had, in his own terms, succeeded.

But how generally applicable is deconstruction to philosophy? Is there any truth in the suspicion that it might be peculiarly relevant to the supposedly pretentious speculations of European philosophy, but that there is little left in Anglo-American philosophy on which it could feed? This self-congratulatory story does not stand scrutiny. We have only to consider that for Derrida two of his most important predecessors and influences are Nietzsche and Heidegger, and that he seems equally at home deconstructing Austin (and Searle), for the picture to become seriously muddied. Both Carnap and Ayer chose to cite Heidegger as a paradigmatic twentieth-century metaphysician and one could hardly treat deconstruction simply as an antidote to one of its strongest precursors. The explanation for this, of course, is something that neither Carnap nor Ayer cared to mention, namely that Heidegger had his own enormously powerful 'critique' or, better, diagnosis of metaphysics, and it is this that Derridean deconstruction develops.

Could there then be a philosophy that would be resistant to if not totally immune to deconstruction? If the impossibility of the philosophical project arises from the attempted union of the two elements discussed above – the ideal (transparent expression of truth) and the means (writing) – then two deviant options are open, to abandon writing, that is, linguistic expression, or to abandon the ideal. It is perhaps too neat to suggest that Wittgenstein moved from the first option to the second, but there is something in it. The closing remarks of Wittgenstein's *Tractatus* and his remarks on 'Heidegger, Kierkegaard and Ethics'[7] suggest that the truth lies beyond linguistic expression (or at least certain key truths, those concerning the relationship between propositions and facts in the world, and those of ethics). Perhaps more interestingly, it could be said that the Wittgenstein of the *Philosophical Investigations* abandons the ideals constitutive of philosophy. For the therapeutic model is already a self-conscious departure from philosophy thought of as a systematic 'discipline' – indeed it diagnoses the tendencies behind such philosophy as in large part responsible for the problems of philosophy. While for Kant the general error lay in applying empirical concepts beyond their proper sphere, therapeutic philosophy sees perplexity arising when language is disengaged from its proper everyday context of use, when it 'goes on holiday'. And just as language is understood in this essentially practical way, so the solution is practicall. When the perplexity vanishes, the philosophical problem has been solved, even if it is reassuring to have had some insight into how it arose in the first place. This at least would distinguish philosophical therapy from some distraction, or a tranquillizer, or a good night's sleep which might have the same effect. But as I understand it, this insight into the cause of philosophical perplexity, even assuming it to be a condition of the cure, need not be stateable, need not take the form of a true proposition, and certainly need not have any application to the philosophical perplexities that can arise in other languages. Not only is there no need for such a philosophy to institutionalize itself in a more systematic form, it arguably could not do so, because it is just such rigid formulations, such attempts to make language behave in artificial ways that generate philosophical problems. So it would seem that the later Wittgenstein developed a kind of critical philosophical practice that would not be vulnerable to deconstruction. It not only abandons theoretical truth as a goal, it also resembles deconstruction itself in having a general 'theory' of philosophy, and self-consciously forging a counter-philosophical strategy.

I am not the first to have drawn a parallel between Derrida and Wittgenstein.[8] If we were to adopt Rorty's broad brush distinction between systematic and edifying philosophers, and if deconstruction and edification were at all synonymous, then Dewey, Nietzsche, Kierkegaard and the later Heidegger would all join the party, and we would discover that deconstruction was not, as some believe, the name for Derrida's personal style, but the name of a whole submerged tradition in philosophy.[9] Such a view has its dangers, like those involved in making Shakespeare the first existentialist. Deconstruction is an exemplary case of edification in the rough and ready sense Rorty gives to it, but these friendly assimilations can shed a dark light.

For in fact even the Wittgenstein/Derrida comparison soon founders. It is tempting to agree that deconstruction has a therapeutic intent, for if it can be shown both in general and case by case that an extra-linguistic ground of meaning is always illusory, its impossibility marked in any given text by chains of substitution and deferments, then it could be expected to free us from the pain of repeated failure to achieve such an impossible ideal. But does not deconstruction question precisely the wholeness or health towards which therapy would be directed? Deconstruction would be joining a distinguished philosophical tradition (including Russell) if it aimed *to make things more difficult* rather than merely solving problems. Successful therapy can often be achieved by believing a rich and convincing story. The disturbing disillusioning effect of deconstruction is anti-therapeutic, unless one can grasp the nettle of combining a stilling of metaphysical desire with continued fascination at the textual efforts to satisfy it.

This points to a second divergence from the later Wittgenstein. While Wittgenstein may have read more books than was first apparent from his sparse bibliographical apparatus, he never engages in the kind of close textual scrutiny that is Derrida's stock-in-trade. Philosophical problems are presented as arising out of and having to be related back to natural conversational contexts, or language games, and ultimately forms of life. Derrida on the other hand interests himself in those extended textual elaborations that we call classic philosophical works. We could just say that they are doing different things and leave them in peace. We could further explain the difference in terms of Derrida's literary background, and Wittgenstein's assimilation of the tradition of common-sense philosophy which has always had conversation as its touchstone. But the difference cannot be represented as an equable division of the post-metaphysical domain. Extended philosophical discourse – verbal or written – allows the development, or at least the attempt to develop, contexts of significance with a degree of autonomy from everyday discourse. It is this that makes 'fictional truth' possible, as well as mathematical calculation. Even if conversation were in some significant sense the actual empirical starting point for language, which seems unlikely, nothing requires that the constraints of everyday verbal exchange inform every complex organization of language that develops out of it. Indeed everything points in the opposite direction.

Derrida holds two principles: that meaning is always contextual, and that no context is ever saturated, completely determinate.[10] And from these claims follows a claim about general semantic indeterminacy which serves to further distinguish Derrida's position from Wittgenstein's. We can attribute the first principle to Wittgenstein but not the second. The whole point of Wittgenstein's references to 'language games', and ultimately 'forms of life', is to set limits to that release from essentialism enshrined in 'don't look for the meaning, look for the use'. It involves a privileging of normal, standard use over literary (or philosophical) use, a privilege strengthened by associating the normal use with the practical, the everyday engagement of language in our life (as gears are *engaged*). Here we are supposed to meet determinate and determinable contexts, settings in which language thrives in natural health.

I do not know anywhere that Derrida has discussed Wittgenstein. But a Derridean reading of Wittgenstein would surely bring out the structure of release and retention (Freud's discussion of the Fort/Da game would present a parallel) in which context supplies what definitions cannot. It would bring out the tacit decision to, in effect, distinguish conversational contexts from literary and other 'textual' ones, and to privilege the former. It would argue that it is via a succession of distinctions and valuations that 'contexts' are determined – both in practice and in philosophical reflexion – but that such determination involves an exclusion (repression) of the realms of imagination, fantasy, unlikely but possible outcomes, dream, etc. Where Wittgenstein would talk about language games, Derrida would talk about 'play'.[11] If on Wittgenstein's view language is engaged as gears are engaged, there is, for Derrida, irreducible play in the linkage. The play is not located simply in the possibility that an apparently serious and straightforward utterance may have been meant ironically, or as a *double entendre*, or poetically. Rather the very possibility of forming any simple or complex intention is the possibility of repeating a phrase that has acquired its semantic load in innumerable other contexts, some 'literary', others whimsical, yet others 'purely practical', and there is no possibility of focusing and completely mastering the sense it has acquired.[12]

Deconstruction resists appropriation by the tradition. But equally, that tradition lives on, either oblivious to or disdainful of this critical method. Why? Philosophers can be roughly divided up into those with some sympathy for things continental, and those with very little. Those with very little sympathy will be repelled by Derrida's fancy footwork, his inability to get to the point, to say clearly what he is doing and do it. Most of those with such sympathies have come to identify themselves with phenomenology, existentialism or continental Marxism and have considerable intellectual investment in these areas. Derrida poses enormous difficulties for each of these positions, and in terms that these scholars often prefer to ignore.

But these are explanations, not reasons. Is it possible to construct a good case against taking deconstruction seriously, let alone actually practising it? I would like to distinguish two sorts of objections: 'theoretical' and (loosely) 'moral' or 'practical'. From a theoretical point of view, one might claim that the practice of deconstruction is self-defeating, that is, is based on a mistaken theory of language, over-generalizations about philosophy, or some other factual or logical error. From a 'moral' point of view, one might claim that whatever the theoretical basis, deconstruction is destructive of values, it is debilitating and discouraging, that it saps philosophical initiative. In short it is an intellectual scourge.

Most sympathetic discussions of deconstruction refute the charge that deconstruction is destructive. Derrida's non-destructive deconstruction has been compared favourably with Heidegger's destructive de-struction. Unfortunately this is doubly misguided, for Heidegger took pains to dissociate himself from any destructive intent.[13] What is at stake, of course, is what deconstruction does and to what it does it. Deconstruction is above all a way of reading a text, which usually means a way of 'writing on' a text. How does it differ from 'ordinary' readings? We could call interpretation a method of reading (and writing) which aims at bringing out the meaning/message of the text more clearly perhaps (or just in a different way) than the original text. It might even supply missing premises, explain the author's basic motives, etc. Deconstruction does not do this. Rather than help a text to fulfil itself by bringing out its real meaning, it looks at just those points at which the text subverts itself, at which the attempt at closure (for example, saying just THIS and not THAT) breaks down; it attempts to bring out and subvert the conceptual hierarchies that structure a text. What this does destroy is a certain facade of unity, a certain presumption about what a text is, or should be helped to be. But equally, it could be said to bring to life in the text the forces active in its construction. The text ceases to be a thing containing a meaning, but becomes (again) a struggle between order and chaos, a desperate attempt to exchange its own materiality for a transparency.

Deconstruction is destructive, but in no different a sense than philosophy has always been, at least in its 'critical' phase. And yet does not deconstruction destroy philosophy, and so undermine the very critical capacities that we so value? I would rather say that it draws our attention to a level of organization of philosophical texts that transforms our understanding of the philosophical project.[14] It does not 'leave everything as it is', as an early commentator suggested. Indeed perhaps nothing can ever be the same again. But this transformation is in no strong sense destructive. If the moral objection is misdirected, I cannot deny that for some the effect might actually be debilitating and discouraging. But so too was heliocentrism for those who believed that the earth was the centre of the universe.

And so too for some believers is the suggestion that heaven is not a real place.

The second ground for criticism is more serious and more difficult to meet because of the variety of philosophical objections there have been and could in principle be to deconstruction. First there are those who have found fault with particular Derridean readings. Husserlians contest his reading of Husserl, de Man disputes his reading of Rousseau, Searle attacks his reading of Austin, and Derrida's treatment of Marx, Heidegger and Freud have all had their critics. However, even if each of these responses were individually deserved, that would not necessarily constitute a cumulative case against deconstruction because they are each mounted on different grounds. What they do show is more reassuring from Derrida's point of view and ours, that deconstruction is not the philosophical equivalent of turning over the chess board when you are tired of the game. It can and does contribute to the continuation of philosophical discourse.

A second kind of theoretical criticism would dispute one or other of the 'theories' as I have called them, on which the practice of deconstruction is based. Let me enumerate some of the kinds of objections:

(1) That his 'theory' of philosophical discourse, and its historical application to the whole history of philosophy – that philosophy is a self-effacing privileging of 'presence' – is too general to be informative and too simple to be likely to be true.

(2) That deconstruction self-deconstructs because, as he claims, all his deconstructions are themselves deconstructable, because he has to make use of traditional critical philosophical tools to get off the ground, and because his account of *différance* as the productive source of all meaning just repeats the very kind of transcendental argument to which he is opposed.

(3) That his general claim that philosophy since Plato (with the exception perhaps of Leibniz) has privileged the voice and the spoken word goes completely against the actual historical drift away from oral towards written culture.

(4) That his theory of language fails to distinguish relations of meaning from relations of mere association between words.

(5) That his theory of language is that of a bookworm – irremediably text-centred and unable to accord a proper place to language in the world.

I would like here merely to indicate the direction replies to these charges might productively take:

First reply. The claim that 'presence' is the recurrent dream of philosophy – that co-presence with the other (intersubjectivity), immediate experience, intuition, absolute knowledge . . . all embody this value of immediacy – is for Derrida, I would say, a regulative principle. It guides his readings and its justification must be found in the value of these readings, not in abstract arguments for its truth.

Second reply. If the claim that deconstruction self-deconstructs means that as a method it is applicable to its own previous results, this simply shows it is interminable, not self-contradictory. The suggestion may be that it has to affirm the value of, and indeed employ, principles and ploys that it seeks to put in question. It is in fact one of Derrida's central claims that there is no way of avoiding using traditional philosophical arguments and philosophemes; the resulting texts do not so much endorse them as absorb them in a complex strategy.

Third reply. It is said that the historical claim about the traditional privileging of speech is implausible. Certainly when we say 'Can I have it in writing?' we are hardly confirming Derrida's thesis about phonocentrism, but a full answer to this question would have to take into account that the rise in the practical importance of writing since the invention of mathematics, since the keeping of records, since the invention of the printing press, is quite compatible with a philosophical sense that the advent of writing – marks cut adrift from their original intentional matrix – is a moment of crisis. The sense of semantic transparency, of directly knowing what one means when one is aware of oneself speaking, is lost. There is no incompatibility between the decline in the actual importance of speech, and a perpetuation or even an augmentation of its value. (Think of the contemporary value placed on the 'natural' which coincides with the increasingly problematic status of 'nature'.) And a philosophical response to Derrida's thesis here would have to offer alternative yet convincing accounts of the hostility to or ambivalence about writing that Derrida finds in Plato, Rousseau, Hegel, Saussure and Husserl. We must also bear in mind what could be called one of Derrida's deconstructive *theses*, that speech is itself a form of writing, that is, that the supposedly deficient predicates usually attached to writing (for example, not being under the conscious control of the producer of signs) apply equally to speech.

Fourthly, it is said that Derrida ignores the distinction between meaningful and associative relations between signs.[15] But we ought perhaps to focus more sharply on the word 'ignore'. Did Quine *ignore* the analytic/synthetic distinction? Does Nietzsche *ignore* the fact/value distinction? Scruton's claim is quite misleading. It suggests the condescending attitude that these French philosophers may have their hearts in the right place but in terms of ability to make crucial distinctions they desperately need our help. The fact is, of course, that Derrida systematically questions the distinction between relations of meaning and relations of association. One of the key strands in the argument, for example, is that relations of meaning are 'ideal' and that such 'ideal' relations are never in fact realized. The word 'ideal', we might say in analytical vein, functions like 'imaginary' and 'non-existent'. Even if we understood the strongest relation of meaning – synonymy – as substitutability in all contexts *salva veritate*, the actual identification of a single synonym could only ever happen . . . tomorrow.

Derrida, it is true, exploits this blurring of association and meaning to extremes. I discuss in Chapter 2, 'Metaphysics and Metaphor', the semantic skating and skidding he indulges in in his paper on metaphor, 'The *retrait* of metaphor',[16] in which he takes the tenor/vehicle distinction as the occasion for a tour of the language of transportation. And yet in this playing around he manages to bring to life not only the etymological sense of metaphor, but a whole range of terms – usually themselves metaphorical – that have been used to characterize metaphor.

Fifth reply. The text-centredness objection ('Il n'y a pas de hors-texte'). But what is a text? Or the text? There are two different answers to this question, even in Derrida, and corresponding to these different answers there are two different claims being made when he says there is nothing outside the text. In the first sense of text, we are talking about something that might containably be called Rousseau's text, or Derrida's text. The individuation of a text in this sense is not, as it usually is for a book, simply an empirical matter. What is at stake is the unity of a certain signifying structure. In one of his chapters on Rousseau, Derrida writes:

> The writer writes in a language and in a logic whose proper system, laws and life by definition his discourse cannot dominate absolutely. He uses them only by letting himself, after a fashion and up to a point, be governed by the system. And the [deconstructive] reading must always aim at a certain relationship, unperceived by the writer, between what he commands and what he does not command of

the language he uses. This relationship is not a certain quantitative distribution of shadow and light of weakness or of force, but a signifying structure that critical reading should *produce*.[17]

If the boundaries of a text may coincide with a book or books, or a collection of parts of books, 'text' is understood as a signifying structure, not an object in the world. Assuming for a moment that we can indeed individuate texts in this way, by reference to the boundaries of a writer's discourse, to a containable signifying structure, then the claim that there is nothing outside the text means that texts themselves have the capacity to anticipate, to articulate, the very relation between what lies inside and outside them. Derrida explains this, as we have seen, via the logic of supplementarity, by which he demonstrates a parallel, and perhaps convergent, chain of substitutive connections which in Rousseau's texts link speech to writing, and sex to masturbation. In each case there is a contradictory or paradoxical (unthinkable to reason) relation in which something defined as being complete is none the less brought to completion by what exceeds and even threatens it. In each case, nature, posited as preceding culture, is in fact completed by it, and this is a truth about writing, textuality and signifying structures in general.

> In what one calls the real life of these existences of flesh and bone [Derrida is talking about Rousseau himself, and Therese and Mamma], beyond and behind what one believes can be circumscribed as Rousseau's text there has never been anything but writing; there have never been anything but supplements, substitutive significations which could only come forth in a chain of differential references, the 'real' supervening, and being added only while taking on meaning from a trace and from an invocation of the supplement, etc . . . And thus to infinity, for we have read in the text that the absolute present, Nature, that which words like 'real mother' name, have always already escaped, have never existed; that what opens meaning and language is writing as the disappearance of natural presence.[18]

Writing generates a nostalgia for a sense of the natural which is actually dependent on writing as its transgression. Derrida is not *advocating* a text's anticipation of its own outside, a kind of textual idealism, he is diagnosing structures of textual signification, of which philosophical texts are the finest examples, which mistakenly encourage such metaphysical interpretations.

There is however a second and different claim being made under the rubric that there is nothing outside the text, which involves a generalization of the concept of 'text'. He wrote recently, 'For strategic reasons . . . I found it necessary to recast the concept of text by generalizing it almost without limit. That is why there is nothing 'beyond' the text . . . '.[19]

The idea of the general text is one that extends as far as writing extends. And if we understand writing as the articulation of differences, then it would not be opposed to consciousness or experience, but would claim that these themselves would display its primitive structures – differentiation, deferral. Derrida is not so much rejecting or denying consciousness, subjectivity, the real world, etc. as suggesting that in so far as they are significant they come within the domain of writing and textuality. This is not so implausible. If philosophical texts have links to an 'outside' called history, that history, made up as it is of real hard events, has still to be given sense, to be articulated, before it can relate to anything. The reasons for Derrida's increasing contempt for those who insist that 'deconstructionists [should] go beyond the text' become obvious. When this charge originates from followers of Foucault, it is even more misguided. Foucault's 'discursive formations' and the institutional practices with which they are interwoven are precisely what is included in the general text.

I have tried in this last section to suggest ways in which deconstruction can be defended against some of the commonest objections.[20]

There remains one question that full-time professional deconstructors would, I am sure, deem treasonable: in what way if any can we learn from deconstruction without changing horses completely? Can a deconstructive branch be grafted onto a British or Anglo-American rootstock? Indications will have to suffice for now. If we accept something like Rorty's story of the development of twentieth-century philosophy, then Anglo-American philosophy in the hands of Carnap, Sellars and Quine has, by undermining a representational model of knowledge and truth, paved the way for a mode of philosophizing that would at least share with deconstruction a kind of meta-scepticism about traditional philosophical goals. Whether displacing or fracturing traditional philosophical texts would bulk large in what Rorty calls the continuing 'conversation of the West' I do not know.

There is a simpler and more straightforward sense in which Derrida's deconstruction can be seen as performing, albeit in a different idiom, the same kind of service (if that is what it is) as Quine's critique of the analytic/synthetic distinction, with the important difference that the epistemological requirements of natural science are not calling the tune.

Reading Derrida brings about an acute sensitivity to the figural and metaphorical dimensions of philosophical writing. 'Metaphor', as we saw in the last chapter, can come to seem not just one philosophical topic among others, but to play a pervasive role in the construction of philosophical arguments. One is then faced with the need to come to terms with the possibility that metaphor (and indeed other forms of equivocation, ambiguity, figurality and semantic indeterminacy) might be ineliminable in principle from philosophy.[21]

Finally, Derrida raises anew questions which must not be seen as diversions with which 'practical thinkers' ought to be impatient about the values and goals of philosophy. We may not agree with the universal application of his diagnosis of philosophy as an impossible project, and much of his recent work (for example, on friendship) suggests he has found productive ways of carrying on.[22] But equally, a complacent falling back to a therapeutic grasp of the philosopher's activity is not possible because of the aporias latent in the goals of therapy itself. Derrida, moreover, has demonstrated that, by the development of subtle strategies, one can more or less 'successfully' perform what might seem an impossible operation, the turning of philosophy's natural scepticism onto its own structure, its ruses and its goals. And this possibility continues to be worth exploring.

Notes

1 See his 'Limited Inc abc', *Glyph*, vol. II, 1977, and 'Racism's Last Word', in *Critical Inquiry*, autumn 1985, p. 292.

2 For a very different account see Louis Sandowsky's '*Différance* beyond phenomenological reduction', in *Warwick Journal of Philosophy*, vol. 2, no. 2, autumn 1989.

3 Indeed this is the basis for de Man's critical discussion in 'The rhetoric of blindness: Jacques Derrida's reading of Rousseau', in *Blindness and Insight*, (London: Methuen, 1983).

4 See his *Speech Acts* (Cambridge: Cambridge University Press, 1972). It is with Searle that Derrida has had his most celebrated 'exchange' (see note 1 to 'Limited Inc abc').

5 See Chapter 3 of Christopher Norris, *The Deconstructive Turn* (London: Methuen, 1983).

6   In his *Margins of Philosophy* [1972] (Brighton: Harvester Press, 1982).
7   'This running up against the limits of language is ethics ... In Ethics one is always making the attempt to say something that does not concern the essence of the matter, and never can concern it' (1929).
8   The most fully worked account is by Henry Staten, *Wittgenstein and Derrida* (Lincoln: University of Nebraska, 1984).
9   See, for example, Mark Taylor, *Deconstruction in Context* (Chicago: University of Chicago, 1986).
10 I owe this formulation to Jonathan Culler, *On Deconstruction* (London: Routledge, 1983).
11 The French word is of course 'jeu', which can also mean game, and has sometimes been translated, not unproblematically, as 'free-play'. I owe this observation to discussions with Marian Hobson.
12 Definition and stipulation would be mere symptoms of a desire not examples of successful restriction of meaning.
13 See section 6 of his *Being and Time* [1927], trans. Macquarrie and Robinson (Oxford: Blackwell, 1962).
14 This has been systematized by Rodolphe Gasché as a theory of infrastructures in his excellent *The Tain of the Mirror: Derrida and the Philosophy of Reflection* (Cambridge: Harvard, 1986).
15 Roger Scruton made this claim in a broadcast review of *Deconstruction and Criticism*.
16 'The *retrait* of metaphor', *Enclitic*, vol. II, no. 2, fall 1978.
17 *Of Grammatology* [1967] (Baltimore: Johns Hopkins, 1976), Part II, Chapter 2, p. 158.
18 ibid., p. 159.
19 The full text of this angry riposte to straw-headed critics can be found in *Critical Inquiry*, autumn 1986, p. 167.
20 A fuller response to such doubts and objections can be found in my 'Beyond deconstruction?', in A. Phillips Griffiths (ed.), *Contemporary French Philosophy* (Cambridge: Cambridge University Press, 1987), pp. 175–94. My fifth reply draws heavily on this paper.
21 This is a direction taken by much contemporary interest in metaphor, a direction that could perhaps re-read with profit the suggestions about a finite number of generative 'root metaphors' made by Stephen Pepper in his *World Hypotheses* (Berkeley and Los Angeles: University of California Press, 1942).
22 See, for example, his *Memoires for Paul de Man* (New York: Columbia 1986); and 'The politics of friendship', *Journal of Philosophy*, vol. 85, no. 11, Nov. 1988, pp. 632–44.

Further reading

The relation between deconstruction and criticism depends a lot on how one understands 'criticism'. It has been understood in a literary way (linked to 'literary criticism' and 'literary theory'), it has been thought of in some general connection to a critical philosophical method, and it has been understood more narrowly to invoke a relation to the critical theory of the Frankfurt school. The first sense captures the orientation of Harold Bloom *et al.* (eds), *Deconstruction and Criticism* (New York: Seabury, 1979), something of a statement of the Yale school, and including a paper by Derrida on Blanchot (and Shelley), 'Living on: border lines'. See also Vincent Leitch, *Deconstructive Criticism* (London: Hutchinson, 1983); Geoffrey Hartman, *Saving the Text* (Baltimore: Johns Hopkins University Press, 1981); Jonathan Culler, *On Deconstruction* (London: Routledge, 1983).

The contribution of deconstruction to a more general critical philosophical method is made more complex by the vulnerability of the very idea of 'critique' to deconstructive treatment. Perhaps the most interesting work in this area has been done by Rodolphe Gasché, first, in his essay 'Deconstruction as Criticism', in *Glyph 6* (Baltimore: Johns Hopkins University Press, 1979), which considers Merleau-Ponty and Deleuze as precursors of deconstruction, and his splendid *The Tain of the Mirror: Derrida and the Philosophy of Reflection* (Cambridge, Mass.: Harvard University Press, 1986). Gasché is concerned to rescue Derridean deconstruction for philosophy from its deployment in a (merely) literary context, an endeavour pursued for example by the collection by John Sallis (ed.), *Deconstruction and Philosophy* (Chicago: Chicago University Press, 1987). Richard Rorty's 'Philosophy as a kind of writing', in *The Consequences of Pragmatism* (Brighton: Harvester, 1982) is another serious philosophical appreciation. From a quite different direction, deconstruction has come in for much negative assessment from those committed to critical theory. Habermas devotes Chapter 7 of *The Philosophical Discourse of Modernity* (Cambridge, Mass.:The MIT Press, 1987) to a rather feeble discussion of Derrida. A more sustained and wider criticism of French Nietzscheanism (including Derrida) can be found in Peter Dews's, *The Logics of Disintegration* (London: Verso, 1988).

More generally on deconstruction, there are a number of recent books by Christopher Norris: *The Deconstructive Turn* (London: Methuen, 1983), *The Contest of Faculties* (London: Methuen, 1985) *Derrida* (London: Fontana, 1987), with a good bibliography; and *Deconstruction and the Interests of Theory* (London: Pinter, 1988); there is John Llewelyn's more advanced *Derrida on the Threshold of Sense* (London: Macmillan, 1986) and D. C. Wood and R. Bernasconi (eds), *Derrida and Différance* (Evanston, Ill.: Northwestern University Press, 1987).

4

Philosophy as writing:
the case of Hegel

There seem to be at least three quite different ways of understanding philosophy *as* literature, having first made the assumption that we are dealing with works of philosophy not already securely tagged with the label literature. I will call them evaluative, descriptive and revisionary.

By an evaluative approach, I mean one that fastens on the aesthetic merits of a philosophical text in whole or in part. We might look at Plato's use of myth, for example, from a literary point of view. We could note that Hume's *Dialogues on Natural Religion* are brilliantly written and show how. We might say of Hegel, as British commentators once did, that reading him was like wading through deep mud with heavy boots on. We might praise Russell's clarity. These would all be evaluative approaches to the literary merits of philosophical writing. However interesting this is, I shall not indulge in it.

By a descriptive or analytical approach to philosophy as literature, I mean a study which, whether or not it commits itself to a normative judgement is concerned to describe in detail a philosopher's style, the construction of his work, how he produced his literary effects. Its limitation is that it maintains a strict distinction between what a philosopher is saying and how he says it, concerning itself only with the latter.

The revisionary approach knows no such boundaries. It too is concerned with the functioning of the text, with how effects are produced. But its aim is the deconstruction of texts to the point at which philosophical effects are themselves seen as the product of a practice of writing or identical with it.

The fact that these options can be analytically distinguished from one another in no way guarantees agreement among the practitioners

67

of any one of them. The revisionary approach in particular raises all sorts of questions to which there seems to be no simple *a priori* answer, and consequently no guarantee that its advocates will share a single voice.

Rather than attempt any general resolution of the problems raised by the revisionary approach, I shall simply try to clarify two of them. If we suppose that philosophy can be absorbed into 'literature' and that somehow, like one of those egg-eating snakes, literature does not choke on it, we none the less put the meaning of 'literature' in question because there are differences between *Sense and Sensibility* and *Sense and Sensibilia* which cannot be ignored. The second problem is that this whole revisionary project, itself a form of writing, places its own status in question. Some would see it as another phase in the historically developing self-criticism of philosophy. But again, there is no obvious *a priori* answer here; the time is ripe for a certain risk. One risks error, but I am not the first to think that the fear of falling into error is the prime error.

Even if there is no certainty of victory in the argument, it is worth sketching the form that a skirmish might take between the revisionary approach to philosophy as literature and someone who believed in the autonomy of philosophy. Such a person would see in this project an old enemy, reductionism, returning in different cloth. His strongest argument against this whole project – that it is itself nothing but a philosophical project, because of the philosophical presuppositions it makes – is however, a very dangerous one, because to claim that it misunderstands itself, and that the revisionist is really a philosopher, is to be forced to take him seriously! The other most promising move would be to claim that the sort of translation rules by which the revisionist could translate philosophy into some other discourse – literature, or some sort of neutral 'writing' – that these rules do not exist, just as there are no rules for translating brain process descriptions into mental state descriptions. But this objection involves both an excessive demand and a misunderstanding. The excessive demand is that the rules be exhibited before the programme has been properly launched, and the misunderstanding is to suppose that the rules are just there waiting to be discovered. Reductionism creates rules, it performs translations, it does not meekly wait for them to be authenticated and approved by some official body. So even if my position were mistaken for a form of reductionism there would be answers to those who objected to it as such.

If I am right in thinking there is a distinct and defensible approach to the understanding of philosophy which involves treating it as some sort of literary construction, what are its particular merits? Is it important that we adopt it rather than some other method? I will try to explain why I think the answer to this last question is yes.

I will first argue a general case for analysing philosophical texts in this way, and then I will make out a case for doing so at this historical juncture.

Like literature, philosophy is not distinguished from other subjects by a specific approach to a subject-matter independent of it. Chemistry deals with chemicals, biology with life and astronomy with very large, very distant objects. Philosophy can boast no such definite subject-matter. One might think there was an analogy here with the fact that one can write a novel about anything. In each case, what distinguishes these types of achievement is their form. And in both cases this form is written.

An exploration of the boundary between philosophy and literature and the methods deployed in each is justified as soon as one realizes that there is nothing fixed about it. History has witnessed considerable changes in what counts as philosophy, and there is still no consensus. Moreover the choice of a constituency for establishing any consensus would itself be a philosophically important matter. Should one choose academic philosophers, or men and women in the street? Quite apart from what most people suppose philosophy to be, it is a question every philosopher asks explicitly or in practice.

But if it has always been possible to see philosophy as writing, why has it now become a compelling question? First, there is a revival of interest in systematic philosophers, and if we are not merely to expound their thought, we need a way of handling it critically. That often means handling concepts whose native cultural tradition has disappeared. Second, among those who understand philosophy as ideology, there is a recognition that it is still ideology with a structure, and the analysis of texts as structured products is a good antidote to crude materialism.

Third, there is a double recognition of, on the one hand, the weaknesses of a linguistic philosophy that is almost entirely concerned with ordinary language (where that means ordinary speech), and, on the other, the ever increasing importance of language, especially with the rapid rise of linguistics. What ordinary language philosophy ignored about philosophy was that the meaning of philosophical concepts has been developed systematically in texts, and that concepts could thereby acquire different characters from the ones they had in everyday conversation. This textual development more easily allowed the over-determination of concepts.

Fourth, philosophical style has again become problematic. Ever since Russell weaned himself from Bradley, English-speaking philosophers have been stressing the importance of clarity. Whenever a French or German book is reviewed in the journals (if it gets there at all) one can expect a patronizing reference to clarity or a tired reference to obscurity sheltering somewhere in the lines. But not only is what we call clarity as often as not putting a brave face on pedantry or banality, it is also a heavily loaded term. There is every reason to believe that clarity as a value rests on a theory of meaning that would wither were it exposed to the light of day. Clarity, a metaphor we might remember, is as obscure as it is problematic. Its use as an overriding consideration when reading or writing philosophy has not been wholly beneficial.

Lastly, the rejection by some linguisticians of the possibility of a logical reconstruction of natural languages, and consequently of arguments expressed in natural languages, has encouraged people to look for more complex rules and construction principles not only in ordinary speech (speech-act theory, pragmatics) but also in writing.

These are just a few of the reasons for treating philosophy as a kind of writing, and inaugurating a critical programme of reading philosophical texts. There are other reasons why this will become a more common practice which relate to the translation of models for imitation from the French, but this may be a symptom as much as a cause. I hope at least enough has been said to arouse interest in the project. I would like here to take an example of philosophical writing, that of Hegel, focusing largely but not entirely on *The Phenomenology of Spirit* [1807] (hereafter *PS*), and see what we can learn by treating it primarily as a text.

There have been a number of attempts to compare philosophy with literature. However closely the two are drawn together, it is not uncommon to insist that the difference lies in the way in which philosophical writing obeys a norm of truth. And what , we might ask, is truth? Truth as a mapping between text and world would seem a bad bet because of the difficulties in independently identifying the philosophical features of the world to which the text is supposed to correspond. One is tempted to an account of truth as consistency, or coherence. But novels can be coherent without being philosophy, and without claiming truth. What is wrong with coherence as a condition

70

is its superficiality. It takes little account of the *depth* of the text. Now 'depth' can be given many different senses. The sense attached to it here is best linked to a feature of philosophical thinking that has never been disputed, that philosophy is reflective, and indeed self-reflective. I claim that this can serve as a partial criterion for the identification of texts as philosophical, without any speculation about the author's state of mind.

But this does not tell us where in a text to look for reflexivity, for the good reason that there is no rule about where it must occur. But this does not mean we cannot pin it down in particular texts, nor does it prevent us from outlining patterns of reflexivity of wider application.

In the case of Hegel, I would like to show that there are at least three modes of what I am calling textual reflexivity, by virtue of which the text is governed by the norm of truth. The first mode I will call exemplification, the second reflective modification, and the third, with some terminological reservations, totalization.

Exemplification is in fact a hydrated term swollen with many meanings. It designates a structure that can appear in many guises.

Many philosophical texts contain terms or concepts which are to be understood not just 'in context' but in the way their meaning actively informs or structures the text. This may occur at any or all of a number of different levels. To take a trivial example, the term *thesis* may occur in a book, the whole argument of which we might call a thesis, and also refer to or be exemplified in the concluding or opening sentence of the book in which the central thesis is spelled out. In this case, the term thesis is doubly exemplified. Consider now the claim that the term 'dialectic' in Hegel's writing was over-determined. This can be understood as the claim that dialectic is multiply exemplified in his writing. The same point could be put in other ways, by referring to internal referentiality, or internal textual intentionality. The important thing is the way in which such terms both occur in the text, and operate in it by being exemplified in it, at other levels. I will call such terms operators, of which there are at least three kinds.

Firstly, there are boundary regulators, that organize from within the relationship between the particular text and what lies outside it (for example, other texts, other forms of knowledge). Hegelian examples of such regulators would be the terms 'philosophy', 'absolute' and 'science', each of which allows the text to determine from within, albeit in different planes, its own location.

The second sort of operator is what I call a structural operator. Such terms are exemplified in the internal structure of the text.

Hegelian examples of structural operators include such terms as 'stage', 'moment', 'truth' and 'language', in the tacitly plural contexts in which he talks about 'the truth of', 'the language of'. Such structural operators indicate a reflective exemplification at the level of the middle range structure of the text.

Finally, I would point to transformational operators. These terms are exemplified in the dynamics of the text. Again, Hegelian examples would be 'mediation', 'reflection' and 'negation'. (They correspond to notions like deduction, inference and substitution in formal logic.)

Each of these types – boundary regulators, structural and transformational operators – are types of concepts occurring within the text in which they are exemplified. Not all terms are so exemplified. But it is characteristic of philosophical texts that they contain operators in this sense. These terms could be said to be given their meaning in this way, which is very different from merely being defined in the text. But the word 'meaning' is very worn coin. Better: don't look for the meaning look for the exemplification.

But exemplification has a wider application than the relationship between concepts and the texts within which they are embedded. If we allow that texts contain theories, claims and accounts of things, then exemplification may also be found in the relationship between such theories and the texts in which they are deposited. This is a theoretical vein that I would like to mine in some detail in relation to Hegel's accounts of language and the ways they relate to his own writing.

One of the fascinating aspects of his writing, if one considers together the *Phenomenology of Spirit* [1807], the *Science of Logic* [1812–16] and the *Encyclopaedia* [1830], is the pervasiveness of his concern with language and the way this concern is stratified. At four different levels Hegel makes theoretical remarks about language, each exemplified by his actual philosophical practice.

These four different levels can be distinguished as follows:

(1) Hegel's theory of signification, covering the relationship between intuitions, symbols and signs.
(2) His account of the relationship between speech and writing and of the superiority of alphabetic writing over hieroglyphic writing.
(3) His numerous claims about language as the proper medium of truth, and about different languages or ways of using language characteristic of different stages of the development of spirit (*Geist*).

(4) His remarks about the difference between philosophical and ordinary language.

I claim that the way in which his texts embody or exemplify these different theories about language is one of the most important deep structures of his writing. It allows the text to function as a local demonstration of the truth of its own claims.

In addition to exemplification, there are two other forms of textual reflexivity of equal importance – reflexive modification and totalization.

By reflexive modification I mean the way in which philosophical texts in particular, though perhaps not exclusively, proceed by reflection on themselves. The continuity of a descriptive novel is standardly based on credible event continuities. But philosophical writing is always potentially if not actually self-generative. The way one draws a conclusion from an argument is only one of many forms of reflexive modification. This category would include drawing out the consequences of what has already been written, translating a complex claim into other terms, as when one summarizes a result, or spells out the message. Indeed it covers all occasions on which the principle of textual progression rests on the transformation of part of what has previously been written into an object of further reference. If I were now to have written 'Let me explain what I mean' this would have been an unequivocal example of reflective modification. The concept of reflective modification would enjoin one to look for the actual principles by which a particular philosophical text transforms itself. It is not entirely fortuitous, but the most celebrated example of such textual productivity is to be found right on our doorstep in the concept of the dialectic as Hegel developed it.

Language is an issue for Hegel at a number of different levels, and each of these levels reflects the others. There is a successive embedding between his theory of language, his account of philosophical language and his use of language.

Beginning with Hegel's remarks in Part 3 of the *Encyclopaedia* ('The Philosophy of Mind') we find an explicit theory of language which can be compared with the theory implicit in our central text – the *Phenomenology of Spirit*. What is striking from the outset is his association of the development of language with the rejection of immediacy, with intelligence, and with freedom. In the section 'Theoretical Mind', we are led from recollection, through various stages of imagination to what he calls productive memory. Recollection is the bringing into consciousness of the contents of what he calls a 'night-like mine or pit in which is stored a world of infinitely many images and representations, yet without being in consciousness'.[1] Until I become conscious of these images, I have no control over them, and they are not properly mine. The educated man is the man who does not live in immediate intuition, but in his recollection so that little is new to him any longer. That is because he has brought into consciousness the content of his past impressions. And indeed the first stage of the imagination – reproductive imagination – is characterized by its freedom to recall images, in contrast to the earlier stage in which images are inaccessible to the intelligence.

It is not until we have been through associative imagination and arrived at productive or creative imagination that we reach the point at which images become symbols. But such symbols still represent what he calls 'a conditioned, only relatively free activity of intelligence' (*Enc.*, p. 212), because there is still a residually natural relation between what we would call signifier and signified. The transition to sign proper, as Saussure stressed, appears with the arbitrariness of the sign. Hegel writes: 'The sign is some immediate intuition, representing a totally different import from what naturally belongs to it; it is the pyramid into which a foreign soul has been conveyed, and where it is conserved' (Enc., p. 212).

The process of sign-creation, the privilege of what he calls productive memory, provides the intelligence with intuitions without natural content. And such intuitions are the true property of the intelligence, and constitute the basis of its freedom. Hegel laments the neglect of the study of signs and language, and stresses the need to show 'their necessity and systematic place in the economy of intelligence' (*Enc.*, p. 213). If this clarifies the sense in which the appearance of the sign brings with it a new freedom – from the sensory content of intuition – it also has another effect. Whereas the natural intuition is 'something given, and given in space', it acquires, when employed as a sign, 'the peculiar characteristic of existing only as superseded and sublimated' (*Enc.*, p. 213). This points to the temporality of the sign, by which I think he means that the sign has effects beyond the time of its own existence. The words I have just uttered are no longer, but structure the very sentence I have yet to complete.

So at the base level of the sign, Hegel already understands language in three ways: as inaugurating a new level of being, as giving to intelligence a new freedom, and as transcending the spatiality of natural intuition.

We have not yet established whether Hegel is talking about writing when he talks about signs, or whether he is talking about speech. And what he might mean by either.

He certainly understands speech as having historical primacy over writing. But he stresses that what was peculiar about human speech was that it was articulated, and if originally the different vowels and consonants had some meaning associated with the bodily postures, or mouth shapings associated with them, this has disappeared almost without trace in the course of civilization.

But how then does he understand the relationship between speech and writing? He certainly appears to exhibit what we might, after Derrida, call a phonocentrist position when he describes written language as 'a further development in the particular sphere of language which borrows the help of an external practical activity' (*Enc.*, p. 215). But to suppose that Hegel only thinks of writing as a secondary aid, a supplement, would be mistaken. We can see this from a brief discussion of his views about two different kinds of writing.

It is quite true that the main distinction he draws between hieroglyphic and alphabetic writing is that the former uses spatial figures to designate ideas, whereas the latter uses spatial figures to designate vocal sounds which are already signs. Alphabetic writing, in other words, consists of signs of signs.

His criticism of hieroglyphic language is that it is only suitable for a static civilization like the Chinese. 'Sensible objects no doubt admit of permanent signs . . . [like hieroglyphs] but as regards signs for mental objects, the progress of thought and the continual development of logic lead to changes in the views of their internal relations and thus also of their nature' (*Enc.*, p. 215). And for this an alphabetic language is much more suitable. Hegel then goes on to tie up the fate of vocal language with that of alphabetic writing, and the original dependence of alphabetic on vocal language seems to be reversed: 'The progress of the vocal language depends most closely on the habit of alphabetic writing; by means of which only does vocal language acquire the precision and purity of its articulation' (*Enc.*, p. 216). And if we thought that precision and purity were simply surface phenomena, he immediately associates the use of alphabetic writing with a process which seems essential for the construction of a philosophical text: 'Alphabetic writing is on all accounts the more intelligent: in it the *word* – the mode peculiar to the intellect, of uttering its ideas most worthily – is brought to consciousness and made an object of reflection' (*Enc.*, p. 216).

If we suppose that Hegel still holds to the claim that writing is just a process of making signs of signs, how can it affect speech in the way that he claims it does? And how can he attribute to alphabetic writing the autonomous power to facilitate conscious reflection? I understand Hegel to be describing the role of writing in the production of texts, and I will try to show how this autonomous freedom, exhibited in time and involving a systematic diffusion of immediacy, which we have traced to his most basic reflections on language, is to be found repeated more explicitly at higher levels of the text, and indeed in the practice of writing that we shall call dialectic.

I have so far tried to summarize Hegel's bare theory of language without venturing to wonder whether we might not use the word 'language' in the plural. In his youth, however, Hegel had been much affected by the views of those who, like Herder, understood a language to be expressive of a whole people. This naturally leads to the idea of different languages expressing different cultures, or states of civilization. But what is to count as a language? We have already seen that the Chinese language was thought well matched to the static civilization of ancient China. But it was not the terminology of the language, but its form of writing that was special. And I think Hegel was quite prepared to extend his original insight about languages being culturally expressive from the original claim about natural languages and particular cultures to ways of using a given language, to which would correspond particular stages of culture. Indeed, the expressivity of a highly restricted use of language was already the theme of his poem 'Eleusis' (written for Hölderlin) in which he said that to recover the spirit of Greece in words one had to speak with the tongue of angels, and only to the initiated.

This context is helpful for understanding the way in which the later stages of the *Phenomenology* are, by and large, characterized by ways of using language, or, in our broader sense, different languages. This is not to deny that language was also central earlier on in the *Phenomenology*. No one who has read past the first few pages will have failed to notice the role that language plays in the critique of simple sense-certainty. But at that point his concept of language has not left the level of the word, whereas his later talk of different languages operates at higher levels of linguistic articulation.

Language plays a crucial role in the *Phenomenology* because it mediates the process of reflection between one self-conscious being and another. Language transforms what is inner by allowing expression.

But expression is never simply a making outer of what is inner. For in making it outer, the inner is first conditioned by the medium of expression and second transformed into a self-consciousness existing for others. This process, in which, by language, an individual can reflect on and reincorporate the fact of his or her existence for others, is understood as nothing other than spirit returning to itself.

The examples one could point to in the later stages of the *Phenomenology* would begin with the section on 'Spirit in Self-Estrangement', in which successive and opposed states of cultural integration and disintegration are described via different languages, which is hardly surprising given that estrangement is itself brought about through language (*PS*, p. 308). Hegel talks of the language of flattery, and of the revealing debate between the language of the alienated soul and the honest soul. The alienated soul's existence consists in 'universal talk and destructive judgement, which strips of their significance all those moments which are supposed to count as the true being and as actual members of the whole, and is equally this nihilistic game which it plays with itself' (*PS*, p. 317).

Faced with this, the honest individual who wants to call a stone a stone and a thief a thief stands no chance. His naive language is sucked into the whirlpool as a mere moment. But it does represent for the alienated soul an ideal of unity which he has yet to recapture. Yet he cannot go back, he must go on. If the naive consciousness demands that the cultured individual withdraw, it cannot mean that he should give up 'the extensive richness of his moments' but that it should 'win for itself a still higher consciousness' (*PS*, p. 319). The language of vanity is incapable of expressing the whole.

Hegel returns to language when he discusses conscience. 'Here again,' he says, 'we see language to be the form in which spirit finds existence. Language is self-consciousness existing for others' (*PS*, p. 395). And the language of conscience has solved the problem of the estranged soul – that of speaking a self-dissolving language.

The same sorts of examples could be given in his discussion of religion as art. The progress from the abstract work of art, through the living to the spiritual work of art runs on linguistic rails. It seems to involve getting the work of art to speak for itself in such a way as to reflect the artist's expressive intentions. And this sets up the problem of the place of language in art.

Hegel does not always tell us what the consequences of a particular stage of the progress of spirit would be in linguistic terms. That is, he does not always spell out what sort of language would be used to express it. And when he does the force of the translation of a moment of spirit into a language is not constant. Sometimes he implies no more than that 'this is what it looks like as a language' and at other times he implies that language is the medium in which the whole process is taking place. It is wrong, for instance, to conclude from the fact that language mediates between individuals that it has no inner role in the individual. Once one has reached the level of linguistic consciousness, the whole game is conducted in language. What varies is whether the moves are expressed or not, and the nature of each expression. But we would be quite wrong to suppose that where Hegel does not explicitly give us a linguistic reading of a stage that none could be given. What we have to bear in mind is that such a reading, whenever it occurs, is itself a practice of language, actually operates in the text, and is not just an optional marginal comment. If we were to be given a translation of the last section, 'Absolute Knowledge', into the language suitable for it, we would in fact be going beyond absolute knowledge, setting up a separation between subject and language which it is one of the self-acclaimed accomplishments of absolute knowledge to have put an end to.

If we take it as demonstrated that the *Phenomenology of Spirit* is a mixture of demonstration and language in action, and of meta-remarks about different uses of and modes of language, we have yet to deal with some of his most important remarks about language, those concerning the specificity of philosophical language. We will interpret these for the light they cast on a textual understanding of Hegel.

As Hyppolite has shown[2] the status of philosophical language was one of Hegel's chief concerns. But I cannot go on to comment on how Hegel's actual writing reflects his views of philosophical writing without explaining how I understand them. These views are appropriately enough to be found in his prefaces and introductions, parts of his books which both are and are not part of them.

I shall begin with a quotation from *Science of Logic* (hereafter *SL*) which anyone who has read Freud's note on the antithetical meaning of primal words will find fascinating. After again criticizing the Chinese language Hegel writes:

It is much more important that in a language the categories should appear in the form of substantives and verbs and thus be stamped with the form of objectivity. In this respect German has many

advantages over modern languages; some of its words have the
further peculiarity of having not only different but opposite meanings,
so that one cannot fail to recognise a speculative spirit the language
in them.[3]

He carries on enthusiastically:

> It can delight a thinker to come across such words, and to find the
> union of opposites naively shown in the dictionary as one word
> with opposite meanings, although this result of speculative thinking
> is nonsensical to the understanding. Philosophy therefore stands in
> no need of special terminology (*SL*, p. 32).

What Hegel is so excited about in such words – *Aufheben* is one
commonly honoured – is that they embody at the lexical level what
is for Hegel a feature of the syntax necessary for philosophical writing.
It is in his syntax that the peculiarity of Hegel's style lies. For having
two especially contradictory meanings gives the single word the same
lack of immediacy of meaning that his reflexive sentences are intended
to generate. At the textual level, this non-immediacy is the main
principle for the generation of the text itself. These contradictory
words clearly enough refuse immediacy, but mediation cannot be
contained in the form of the proposition either. We might think
that in a subject/predicate form, the predicate sets up a relationship
to a subject which modifies the subject, and so destroys any simple
understanding of a name as a pure reference. But Hegel equally
rejects the possibility of reality being represented by propositions.
Propositions are just forms of mediation from which the concept, the
subject, must return again into itself. This cashes out very simply in
the form of the speculative judgement, which is the peculiar means
by which philosophy progresses. In the Preface to the *Phenomenology
of Spirit*, the speculative proposition or judgement is made the subject
of explicit comment. For Hegel, the speculative judgement is a sort
of sentence which does not merely have a subject-predicate form,
but which goes on to involve a reflection on the subject-predicate
relation which modifies the sense of separation that might seem to
have been represented in the subject-predicate form. Might it be that
the notoriously reflexive Hegelian style is nothing but the putting
into practice of a theory about the misleading nature of the ordinary sentence? If the movement of his text as a whole involves the

re-internalization of relationships temporarily seen to be external, the speculative judgement echoes this movement in the smallest units of philosophical thinking. The peculiarity of philosophical language is thus not to be found in a specialist terminology but in a special style, a style that even one of his aggrieved opponents, Kierkegaard, was to imitate, not wholly ironically.

It is this practice of sentence construction that he offers us, suitably understood as 'the turning of the concept back into itself' or as conceptual thinking, which is offered as a substitute for what we might call formal reasoning. Formal reasoning destroys the natural movement of thought, the 'immanent rhythm of the movement of conceptual thought'. He calls it empty, dead, abstract – the same words he uses for Kant's categories. Again, what is appealed to is the self-modifying nature of the speculative judgement, in which, we might say, within the unity of a single thought, the subject is modified and this modification returned to the subject again, to use Hegelian language.

Hegel's whole stylistic strategy here reflects the relationship language is supposed to have to the world. If one wanted one's language to reflect reality, and one thought of reality as fluid, as dialectical, then the simple subject-predicate language might be able to say so – I can after all say 'The world is dialectical' – but my language does not show what this consists in. Not, that is, unless I use ordinary language in a new way. And it is by this ambition to mirror in the shape of his language an articulation of the movement of the real that we have to understand Hegel's use of language.

When Hegel writes about the particularity of philosophical thinking, or writing in relation to ordinary thinking, he tries in his second introduction to *Science of Logic* to explain why philosophical thinking seems to be so difficult. And in his explanation he makes use of the same principle by which he distinguished the symbol from the sign in his theory of signification. There he had said that the symbol, while having an indirect relation to its object, none the less is still sensorily connected to it. But the sign arbitrarily signifies its object, and no such sensory connection is left. It was in this lack of a sensory connection that the freedom of the sign consisted. In the same way, the difference between everyday thinking and philosophical thinking is that everyday thinking is pictorial or figurative. It is stuck at the sensory level, while philosophical thinking abstracts from all sensory content. It substitutes 'adequate notions' for semi-pictorial and material conceptions. Ordinary thinking operates with conceptions which are the *metaphors* of real thought and notions. Philosophy consists in the spelling out of the latent implications of our pictorial thinking, translating it, I would say, into the language of reason. Philosophy in its very act is a process of translation!

I have spent so long on Hegel's various levels of theory about language because they are embedded in or reflect one another, and they are each exemplified in Hegel's practice of writing. They also lead us to the second general principle by which the Hegelian text is structured – that of reflexive modification.

As I understand it, dialectic for Hegel can be most profitably treated as a textual process: its proper locus is in writing, not speech, and its basic principle operates at multiple levels of the construction of his texts. It may well be[4] that we cannot give a formally adequate representation of the dialectic. But those who, like Kaufmann, look at the dialectic and shake their heads, claiming it is not a proper method, but rather something like a vision of the world, completely misplace its mode of existence. The dialectic is nothing if not writing. Nor is this an eccentric interpretation of Hegel. He himself writes in the Preface that 'the dialectical movement likewise has propositions for its parts or elements' (*PS*, p. 40).

But why suppose that the dialectic is to be found properly in writing, not in speech?

The dialectic to be found in spoken dialogue can be understood as a dialectically primitive stage of the dialectic as script, with the transcribed and then invented forms of the dialogue as intermediate instances. What appears in the course of this transformation is very simply the immediacy of speech, and the false starts, the intellectual inadequacies, the impossibility of certain forms of editing and correction, the merely local nature of the reasoning. The most important aspect of Platonic dialogue, for the Hegelian dialectic, is the attempt to use the method of inter-subjective reflection to discover what is universal, to define terms. Spoken dialogue is an advance over mere thought because it allows systematic mutual reflection, in which each utterance is taken up and made the basis for a reply. Consciousness, we might say, goes out of itself in dialogue. But the perfect interlocutor is a fiction. There can be no guarantee of systematic construction by this means, so the living dialogue is replaced by the written dialogue. This is then either a mere transcription of the living, in which case it suffers from its faults, while allowing some correction of them, or it is a literary product, with control over both characters being exercised by the writer. But at that point the need to assign the different parts to two characters disappears. And the writer, Hegel, discovers the freedom of self-controlled textual reflexivity.

It might seem that I have only justified the replacement of dialogue by monologue, in which one speaks two voices, in which he takes the part of the idealized other, but in speech. What licenses the transition from speech to writing? To do this, I will sketch an account of the advance that writing makes over speech from the dialectical point of view.

Briefly, language, whether speech or writing, articulates thought, makes it external, whatever one thinks of its state prior to being externalized. But writing, unlike speech, goes further. It makes *time* explicit. Whereas one has to remember what one has said, or what one's friend has said, writing allows the immediate visual objectification not only of what one has just written, but of what one wrote yesterday. Writing brings about an explicit, accessible, intra-textual referability not to be found in speech. The self-reflection made possible by writing allows one to reorganize one's thoughts on a grand scale after one has once written them. Rewriting is basic to writing in a way that revision is not possible for speech. What one writes may be rewritten, whereas what one says will always in some sense stand. (Think of the artificiality of the judge's order, 'The jury will disregard that remark'.)

Writing understood in its materiality is essential for the production of the sorts of texts Hegel has left us. But he did not just write them, he exploited the dialectical possibilities of writing to the full. In his writing, the creative resurrection of words past is one of the principles of textual continuity. Writing guarantees the possibility of its own multiple objectification and reflection. While one might normally think of such self-conscious activity in mental terms, it can be cashed out directly as a reflective process of textual development.

One of the beauties of taking Hegel's writing as an example is that such remarks could be repeated over and over again. Very many of the psychological remarks that one might be tempted to make about an author can be translated into structural claims about Hegel's texts.

Thus we might say that he adopted his philosophical method and style self-consciously. But a psychological elaboration of this claim is far less appropriate than an account of Hegel's reflections on method in his prefaces, and indeed of the *limits* of any such overview that would short-circuit the textual process. We recall the first paragraph of the *Phenomenology of Spirit*:

> For whatever might appropriately be said about philosophy in a preface – say, a historical *statement* of the main drift and point of view, the general content and results, a string of random assertions and assurances about truth – none of this can be accepted as the way in which to expound philosophical truth. (*PS*, p. 1)

We are back to an earlier problem. If philosophy consists in translating figurative language into speculative language, it is simply not possible to improve access to philosophy by returning to ordinary figurative language, because that very language is entirely unsuitable for reflection, let alone a reflection that would adequately present a whole book to a reader. Whether or not we think Hegel's theoretical dilemma is resolved in practice, it is important to understand from these remarks, the elaboration of which constitute the content of the preface, how he thought of his own book. Briefly he thought its content *unrepresentable*. There is no royal road to knowledge, no short cut either. One can only read the book. For what is important is the textuality of the text, not some supposedly abstractable content.

In his own non-preface (entitled 'Hors Livre') to his *La Dissemination*, Derrida understands Hegel's prefaces, in effect, as having a dialectical relationship to what they preface. They represent the outer (the culture of the time) in the book itself, and they introduce the book into the culture. The prefaces are the traces of what is other than the book within it.

What this importantly brings out again is the sense in which the preface is a limit to the text, indeed even giving us something of the other side of this limit, one that defines not only the boundaries but also, in an important sense, the nature of the content. For, as I have said, it is essential to Hegel's text that it be unrepresentable. It is hard to make this claim precise. There is a sense in which no text is representable, which would make it trivially true of Hegel's texts, and there is a sense in which one can indeed represent Hegel's whole system, let alone an individual text. Did not Stace produce a fold-out diagram of the Hegelian 'system' modelled largely on Hegel's own chapter headings in the *Encyclopaedia*? What is importantly lacking here, and it is something that all representations lack, is *the movement of the text*. Stace's diagram is only adequate as a mnemonic device for those who have already 'been through' Hegel.

So far I have considered Hegel's writing at its own level, as it were. I would now like to look down on it, having tried to make explicit what was never completely thematic in the text itself, its status as writing, and try to approach the *Phenomenology of Spirit* as a unity, as a single text. The point from which I would like to start is the almost undisputed verdict of history that 'Hegel's claim of an achieved totality is unacceptable.'[5] But this claim demands clarification. Are we to suppose that Hegel failed where a later or brighter thinker might have succeeded? I think not. What is being objected to is the very project of 'an achieved totality'. But could what is metaphysically impossible be in some sense *textually* possible? And might it not be that such a textual possibility was responsible for the illusion of metaphysical success? For it is still worth asking how does a text *aim* for completeness? How does it bring about closure from within? How, as a totalizing machine, does the text function? For the pretensions of philosophy, historically speaking and by and large, have been such that the question of how a particular philosopher brings off the feat of completing his writing, of insulating it against the tides of criticism, of totalizing his texts singly and jointly, is of more than passing importance. To those who see such an investigation as formalistic, I must object. Philosophy has traditionally always had a universalizing intention. Hegel's texts are just excellent cases. If we can understand these intentions as inseparable from a particular production of a form of textual totality, then we will have understood something very important about how philosophy, so conceived, is possible.

The *Phenomenology of Spirit* is a self-totalizing text by its combination of three different factors:

(1) *Temporal totalization*: It internalizes time within itself and if time is seen as the condition of possibilities that might rupture the given totality, then these possibilities are already circumscribed by the text.

(2) *Linguistic totalization*: It works the whole range of the express-ible. It begins with what can only be meant and not said, and it ends with what can no longer be transformed into the object of another language – absolute knowledge.

(3) *Teleological totalization*: It represents itself as the adequate completion of a process which knows no outside. The movement towards universality and unity in the cessation of which we recognize the end of the text, is present on the very first page.

Let me expand on these claims. Firstly, metaphysics is only the most shameless form in which philosophy claims timelessness for its conclusions. But it remains a bare assurance until we are given some reason to believe it. What I would call the heroic path is to abolish the effects of time by incorporating time within the text. I have already shown how the dialectic both constitutes the inner structure of speculative judgements and the outer relations between them, and in broad strokes offers us a way of understanding the table of contents of the *Phenomenology*. And I have said that Hegel saw the dialectic here as the articulation of the shape of change itself. If we accepted the dialectic as an adequate expression of the surface structure of all change, then his texts would capture, in that sense, the structure of time. We might suppose that such an interpretation of the *Phenomenology* is over-ambitious. But that would be to underestimate Hegel's ambition. Hegel does not abolish time, but he does domesticate it. Time, understood in our ordinary way is an illusion, an empty intuition: 'Spirit necessarily appears in Time, and it appears in Time just so long as it has not *grasped* its pure Notion, i.e. has not annulled Time.' And of course this is an external and inadequate way for the Notion to know itself. He goes on: 'When this latter grasps itself it sets aside its Time-form, comprehends this intuiting, and is a comprehended and comprehending intuiting.'[6]

The setting aside of its own time-form in absolute knowledge is what I have called the domestication of time. There is indeed change. There are indeed oppositions resolved, transformations, commentaries, but these cash out into mere moments on the way, vital to have gone through but equally vital to have left behind. From the point of view of the text itself, this is quite true, for we do indeed end with a textual resolution in which the body of the book, its past, is devoured. Do we not find, in fact, in the spatio-temporality of the text, a straightforward example of the otherwise paradoxical trace left by the past in the process of mediation, in which the past is at the same time present?

The second mode of totalization is linguistic. If time is thought of as a field of possibility, the capturing of which would be a great philosophical asset, the same can be said of language. There is what I would call a theoretical deep structure to Hegel's use of language, accompanied by a totalizing breadth.

His actual linguistic practice is internally justified firstly by his theory of signification – the sign as the natural field for the operation of intelligence. It is justified by his claims about the privilege of alphabetic writing over hieroglyphic writing, and more importantly by his claims about the supremacy of writing over speech. It is further justified by his claims about the specificity of philosophical discourse. Much of this depth, it is true, has had to be imported from other texts of Hegel, but what is not imported is the critical role of language almost throughout the work – as expression, as the embodiment of truth, as the natural condition of the concept and so on. Language is the touchstone of truth in the *Phenomenology*. To be expressed in language is the passport to philosophical consideration: 'What cannot be uttered, feeling or sensation, far from being the highest truth is the most unimportant or untrue.' In the aggressive self-assurance that all that is worth thinking can be written we find what I would call the project of linguistic totalization.

Finally, a few words about teleological totalization. We can illuminatingly consider the text as a success story, as the satisfaction of a desire that it sets up for itself, as a consummation. The text is a complex mixture of anticipatory excitement and prolonged delay. The development of philosophy as a science consists in the systematic deferment of that final identity with itself that he calls the spirit knowing itself. This process consists only in the relentless spelling out of what is potentially already there in the simplest experience, guided by the achieved standpoint of the self-conscious language user. The text is structured by its anticipation of what is to come. The necessity of its movement arises from the application of principles that already anticipate their conclusion. The repetitive, recursive rejection of sensory content, particularity, externality, difference and separation operates in the light of an assurance that an end is nigh. The unsatisfactoriness of each mere moment can only be understood in terms of a possible denouement. The effect of the *Phenomenology of Spirit* is that of a cathartic satisfaction of the philosophical desire for completeness, for a terminus, for universality. But if there is desire at the heart of the philosophical project, then it too is doomed to repetition. If the practice of philosophy is the writing of fiction governed by a norm of truth, we must ask ourselves whether that norm can be defined independently of the texts themselves. Hegel's idealism rests on the belief that it cannot. 'The true shape in which truth exists can only be the scientific system of such truth' (*PS*, p. 3). If our argument has been successful, we will read this claim as a claim about the textuality of truth. Philosophical truth is not a relation between a proposition or even a set of propositions and some real world. It is a formal feature of a text. It is not just a mobile army of metaphors, metonymies and anthropomorphisms. Hegel did his best to excise these from his writing.[7] It is more an effect of the reflexive structure of the text.

Where, after all this, do we stand on the relationship between philosophy and writing? I have tried in the special case of Hegel to show some of the features of philosophical as opposed to other forms of writing. But the question remains as to whether conclusions reached about Hegel really have much value for philosophy as a whole, especially that philosophy which takes Hegel as a model of how *not* to write.

If we think of Hegel as a metaphysician, and ourselves as somehow free from that taint, we ought to pause at the analysis that Derrida makes of the work of an arch anti-metaphysician – Husserl. As we saw in Chapter 3, Derrida shows that Husserl is in fact committed to a doctrine – Derrida calls it phonocentrism – that is pre-eminently metaphysical. But that we do not write like Hegel does not render us immune to a revisionary critique of our philosophical productions as writing aimed at the production of certain textual effects.

This is, of course, no conclusion, for it raises more questions than it answers. I have given more of a structural than a deconstructive account of Hegel's writing. And I have emphasized the very movement of closure that he himself, at a metaphysical level intended. I have suggested that the achievement is structural and textual rather than metaphysical, although arguably I have not proved this. Surely one would expect successful metaphysical achievement to be mirrored by textual closure: the two are at least compatible. Logically, then, my case is weak. My aim is to plant seeds of understanding about how Hegel was for so long thought to have been successful. It would have been a very different strategy to have tried to show all those ways in which the texts explode, in which they leak out, wander off, open up possibilities of dissemination that they cannot control, while giving the achieved appearance of closure.

Finally, we may ask, how does Hegel so understood relate to the general question of the closure of philosophy, and to recent deconstructive attempts to work on the margins of philosophy? After Hegel, philosophy confronts the possibility of *its own death*, and in some sense *has to do so* if it is to remain the most fundamental kind of thinking: '[T]he life of Spirit is not the life that shrinks from death and keeps itself untouched by devastation, but rather the life that endures it and maintains itself in it' (*PS*, p. 19). But if it *risks* death, it cannot actually allow itself to die. It has to live on, even if transformed utterly, and with a new freedom. It faces the possibility of its death when it comes to understand writing and textuality as its unavoidable conditioning limit. And on this story, a writing that embodies a grasp of these limits, working with them, exploiting them, perhaps even affirming and flaunting them, is the obvious successor to philosophy. And perhaps not wholly distant from laughter.[8]

Notes

1 *Encyclopaedia*, trans. W. Wallace (Oxford: Oxford University Press, 1989), Part 3 ('The Philosophy of Mind'), p. 204. Subsequent page references appear in the text as (*Enc.*).

2 Jean Hyppolite, *Logique et Existence* (Paris: Presses Universitaires de France, 1953). And I have nothing but admiration for his shorter essay on the 'Structure of philosophical language according to the Preface to Hegel's *Phenomenology of Mind*', in R. Macksey and E. Donato (eds), *The Structuralist Controversy* (Baltimore: Johns Hopkins University Press, 1967).

3 *Science of Logic*, trans. A. V. Miller (London: George Allen & Unwin, 1969) p. 32. Subsequent page references appear in the text as (*SC*).

4 This has been argued by Michael Rosen in his *Hegel's Dialectic and Its Criticism* (Cambridge: Cambridge University Press, 1982).

5 Malcolm Clark, *Logic and System* (The Hague: Nijhoff, 1971) p. 3.

6 *The Phenomenology of Spirit*, trans. A. V. Miller (Oxford: Oxford University Press, 1977), p. 487. Subsequent page references appear in the text as (*PS*).

7 A full account of Hegel's relation to metaphor must await another occasion.

8 See Derrida on Bataille: 'From restricted to general economy: a Hegelianism without reserve', in *Writing and Difference* [1967] (Chicago: University of Chicago, 1978).

Further reading

Jean Hyppolite's essay 'The structure of philosophic language according to the Preface to Hegel's *Phenomenology of the Mind*', in R. Macksey and E. Donato (eds), *The Structualist Controversy* (Baltimore: Johns Hopkins University Press, 1972) is one of the few to consider Hegel's use of language alongside his views about language.

Derrida's concerns with textuality and with the 'closure' of philosophy are important to this chapter, though there is a strong vein of plain old structuralism in it. A good way in to these problems would be to read Derrida's *Of Grammatology* (Baltimore: Johns Hopkins University Press, 1976), especially Part I, Chapter 1, 'The End of the Book and the Beginning of Writing', and Part II, Chapter 2, '. . . That Dangerous Supplement'. His writings specifically on Hegel (and the problem of totality, supplementarity, prefaces, inside/outside and so on) include *Glas* (Paris: Galilée, 1974); 'The Age of Hegel', (*Glyph*, vol. 1 [new series], 1986); 'Hors Livre', a preface on prefacing to *Dissemination* [1972] (Chicago: Chicago University Press, 1981); 'Tympan', his 'preface' to *Margins of Philosophy* [1982] (Chicago: Chicago University Press 1982); 'The pit and the pyramid: introduction to Hegel's semiology' (also in *Margins*); and (on Bataille) 'From restricted to general economy: A Hegelianism without reserve', in *Writing and Difference* [1967] (Chicago: Chicago University Press 1978).

A very different way of approaching Hegel as a philosopher of totality, can be found in Kierkegaard's *Concluding Unscientific Postscript* (Princeton: Princeton University Press, 1941).

5

Nietzsche's styles

Philosophical style is an essentially contested field. Only those readers of Nietzsche who lack eyes and ears can escape a confrontation with his style. Those who think him a poet rather than a philosopher do so because of his styles. Those who treat him as an analytic philosopher in disguise have patiently to peel aside the style. And those, again, who treat Nietzsche as a liminal thinker, a philosopher of the limits of philosophy have usually given his style(s) special attention.

It is with this last way of reading Nietzsche that I am most concerned, a way that, far from being the hearth of a cosy agreement, is a site of vigorous debate. And in particular, if you consider the disagreement between Heidegger and Derrida on how to read Nietzsche,[1] it is the question of style that surfaces. One obvious question is this: what if anything can one *do* using style that one cannot achieve without it? If one supposes that philosophy has in some sense exhausted its range of possibility, is the only way forward via stylistic experimentation? Is that how we should explain the writing of Heidegger, Derrida, and perhaps Nietzsche?

One thing that is clear from Nietzsche's writing is that we do not just find 'a writer with style' but one who uses a multiplicity of styles (such as aphorism, polemic, allegory, essay, autobiography . . .). Kaufmann's explanation is unsatisfactory however.[2] He suggests that Nietzsche was trying each style on for size, and that none fitted. Kaufmann cannot see that the multiplication of styles might be an end in itself, because he demands finally an underlying unity to Nietzsche's work. For Derrida, on the other hand, it is the irreducible multiplicity of style that delivers Nietzsche, in part, from metaphysics.

However, while we can leave Kaufmann behind we none the less should not suppose that the only important questions raised by Nietzsche's style or styles are those associated with the limits of philosophy or the closure of metaphysics. If we look at what Nietzsche himself says about his own style, we discover two distinct further claims which are only capable of being partially absorbed by a Derridean reading. I will call these the existential and the semantic claims.

The existential and semantic dimensions to Nietzsche's style(s) can be picked out through short remarks Nietzsche himself makes. Consider for example this passage

> This is also the point for a general remark about my art of style. To communicate a state, an inward tension of pathos, by means of signs, including the tempo of these signs – that is the meaning of every style; and considering that the multiplicity of inward states is exceptionally large in my case, I have many stylistic possibilities – the most multifarious art of style that has ever been at the disposal of one man ... Before me, it was not known what could be done with the German language – what could be done with language in general.[3]

Nietzsche offers us here a quite clear existential interpretation of style. 'The meaning of *every* style is to *communicate* a state, an *inward* tension of pathos.' Style here is no immanent feature of a text, but to be *deciphered* as signs of passion, of suffering, of tension. Language here is a means, an instrument, a vehicle which at the right tempo, may successfully convey something of the inner torments of the soul. Nietzsche's position here seems indistinguishable from that of Kierkegaard when, as we will see in the next chapter he claims that the only true communication is indirect. Both associate this indirectness with literary artistry. Nietzsche all puffed up says 'no-one ever was in a position to squander more new unheard-of artistic devices that had actually been created only for this purpose'. (Squandered, of course, because his artistic seed fell on barren ears.) But Nietzsche must be read closely. He writes of communicating a *state, a tension, inward states*. There is no reference to communicating *himself*, to any sort of communion of souls, there is no falling back into a belief in the unity of these states, transcendental or otherwise. There is no self, no I that he is trying to get across. There is dispersal, fragmentation at the source. When Kaufmann insists on a unity underlying fragmentation, he is being anti-Nietzschean. The self is not only not any sort of thing subject to the constraints of logical rules, it is not even a place subject to standard topographical description.

Nietzsche's existential interpretation of his own style is in many ways a commonplace. With style one personalizes an anonymous language, and what style points back to is something inner and private. Does not this very same concept of style resurface in Barthes when he talks of style as a 'transmutation of a humour'? . . . when he calls it 'a self-sufficient language which has its roots only in the depths of the author's personal and secret mythology, that sub-nature of expression where the first coition of words and things take place'.[4]

One might conclude from Barthes' language that he gives the body a role that Nietzsche does not. But in fact for Nietzsche a connection can be drawn between style and the variety of one's states of embodiment that is quite as explicit. Consider these remarks from the preface to *The Gay Science*:

> A philosopher who has traversed many kinds of health, and keeps traversing them has passed through an equal number of philosophies, he simply *cannot* keep from transposing his states every time into the most spiritual form and distance: this art of transfiguration is philosophy. We philosophers are not free to divide body from soul . . .[5]

If the 'meaning of every style' is to communicate an inward state, 'an inward tension of pathos', we have here an explanation of the diverse forms that *tension* has taken in the pathological journey of his life. Style is a symptom of dis-ease, and whatever unity it may give to a text, whatever force it may have, it owes to its being a transformation, a displacement of a state of human embodiment. A style, on this reading is a metaphor of an embodiment, and the multiplicity of his styles a sign of his multiple embodiment. This, for better or for worse, I am calling Nietzsche's existential interpretation of his own style. The fact that it is *absent* from Derrida's own dealings with Nietzsche's styles is something that will exercise us shortly.

The other remark of Nietzsche's that I would like to expand into an account of the semantic dimension of style is found in an 1884 letter to Erwin Rodhe: 'Look and see . . . if vigour, flexibility and euphony have ever consorted so well in our language . . . *My style is a dance – a play of symmetries of every kind, and an overleaping and mockery of these symmetries.* This enters into the very vowels.' This is written with specific reference to *Thus Spake Zarathustra* (*TSZ*), which he had just finished, but it applies equally to many of his other writings.

On this reading, style not only supplements ordinary language so as to make it capable of existential expression, it also serves in some way to deal with the semantic inadequacy of language. I am using this as an umbrella title to capture a whole range of remarks, complaints, criticisms of language that Nietzsche makes in works at both ends of his career. In particular I think of his early 1873 essay 'Truth and Falsity in Their Ultramoral Sense' (TFUMS), his notes for a course on rhetoric in the same year (winter 1872–3), and numerous remarks collected together in the posthumously edited *The Will to Power* (*WP*).

Nietzsche's basic critical insight is continuous with the empiricist denial that there are any necessary connections in the world, that the world exhibits logical relations in itself. Nietzsche in effect says that the same can be said of language as a whole. We read off structures from language – such as object and property – which are just internal grammatical properties of language. The very application of concepts to the world implies a disregarding of all the differences between the various individual items subsumed under the same term. The truth is that the referential and communicative success enjoyed by a language is a product of a general agreement to see the world the way a particular language depicts it for us. But that is itself a product of needs and desires, and not any sort of independent neutral will to truth. Language is at base, he claims, a lie. Later in *The Will to Power* he says that linguistic means of expression are useless for expressing becoming; it accords with our inevitable need to preserve ourselves, to posit a crude world of stability, of 'things' etc. (*WP*, p. 715).

Now there is a sense in which it is wrong to say that *language* is a lie, or deceives us. It would be *better* to say that we allow ourselves to be deceived by language. We think of language representationally, we understand it too essentialistically, and so on. We suppose, for example, that moral evaluations can be stretched between two opposed and exclusive values – good and evil. Most obviously, then, a style which mocks and overleaps such symmetries will shake up some of our naively realistic ways of thinking about and using language. I think Nietzsche is also committed, as we heard in the reference to *The Gay Science*, to the value of a style which *imitates*, in its rhythm, tempo and tone, the rhythm of the world – becoming rather than being. But finally there is a joyous affirmation of language in its own right, in its autonomy from any referential or representational function, a celebration, through a style that 'dances', as he puts it, of what French philosophers used to call the 'liberation of the signifier'. It is here that we find a positive version of the 'language-as-a-lie' thesis. It is the claim that the original relation of language to the world is not just, negatively, misrepresentation, but positively metaphorical, or more broadly rhetorical. The claim appears in the famous passage in which he describes truth (by which he means here truth as a relationship of representation or correspondence between world and word) as 'a mobile army of metaphors, metonyms and anthropomorphisms, illusions of which one has forgotten that they *are* illusions' (TFUMS).

We see the reference to *illusion* creep back in fast, but the first line is the important one here, for it is repeated in the notes on rhetoric:

What is called 'rhetorical', as the devices of a conscious art, is present as a device of unconscious art in language and its development ... no such thing as an unrhetorical, *natural* language exists that could be used as a point of reference: language is itself the result of purely rhetorical tricks and devices. Language is rhetoric, for it only intends to convey a *doxa* (opinion) not an *episteme* (truth). Tropes are not something that can be added or subtracted from language at will, they are its truest nature. There is no such thing as a proper meaning that can be communicated only in certain particular cases.[6]

Style is a dimension of writing thoroughly interwoven with the rhetorical understood here as the realm of tropes. Irony, for example, spans both dimensions. And style is used by Nietzsche here in two ways: both to *highlight* the claimed rhetorical roots of all language, by, for example, exaggeration – demystification by open explicit performance – and also to *celebrate* the fact, for we must not forget that Nietzsche values artistic affirmation. And there is, in *Zarathustra* especially, an extraordinary poetic productivity and textual power born from the sense of freedom that only a positive rhetorical view of language could have provided.

I now want to raise the stakes somewhat. We have discussed the existential significance of style for Nietzsche, and the way style can overcome the semantic inadequacy of language. I want now to show that if we extract this latter thesis and combine it with a *closure of philosophy* thesis, we open the way to what I have called a *liminal* textuality, which I am attributing to Nietzsche. Fortunately there is no need to import the *closure* thesis into Nietzsche's work. Its exploitation by Heidegger and then Derrida derives from Nietzsche's own versions. There are two versions, which I call the structural and the dialectical.

The structural version can be found in *Beyond Good and Evil*, in which Nietzsche observes 'how unfailingly the most diverse philosophers always fill in again a definite fundamental scheme of possible philosophies. Under an invisible spell, they always revolve once more in the same orbit', an orbit, as he goes on to say, prescribed by 'the unconscious domination and guidance of similar grammatical functions'.[7]

From Nietzsche's Olympian heights, it is clear that philosophers return again and again to problems thrown up by language, such as the problem of the nature of the self, for example, which Nietzsche thinks he is dissolving rather than merely contributing to, when he claims it results from the assumption that 'I' functions as a name. This bewitchment by language appears, he suggests, in metaphysical projections of the subject-predicate structure of grammar. But most importantly perhaps it appears in the way in which the matrix of philosophical possibilities is set up by a collection of tired oppositions – reason and emotion, fact and value, existence and essence, matter and form, subject and object, man and woman, good and evil, etc. These oppositions both supply us, as philosophers, with invaluable analytical tools, and also serve as invisible straitjackets for our thought, unconscious limits by which we are not aware of being bound – a prison-house of language thesis. Philosophy keeps repeating itself, unaware that the rules of the game can be spelled out. And clearly Nietzsche thinks that when this can be done the game is up.

The second dialectical version of the closure thesis is to be found in his account of 'How the Real World at Last Became a Myth' (in *Twilight of the Idols* [*TI*]). Here Nietzsche summarizes the history of philosophy in six stages. In each stage what is at stake is the degree and mode of inaccessibility of the real world, beginning with Plato's position, in which only the philosopher possessed the key, progressing through various stages of distancing and deferment of reality to its final abolition and the recognition that with that abolition, its contrast, the world of appearance(s) is also abolished. The scales fall from our eyes and the age of Zarathustra is at hand. The point is that philosophy is seen to have come full circle, and to have *exhausted* itself. The step beyond philosophy coincides in this case with the implosion of the appearance/reality opposition. But that is Zarathustra's step, not Nietzsche's. Nietzsche, unlike his character Zarathustra, was the author of a number of books.

Nietzsche's problem is how to be a philosopher once one has grasped the finitude of philosophy. One could just affirm that finitude, step back into the circle, and keep playing with the old tokens. But Nietzsche does not do this, or not at least intentionally. (Heidegger's judgement on Nietzsche was that the will to power – the position from which he diagnosed the limits of all previous philosophy as metaphysics – was itself caught up in the circle, and makes Nietzsche 'the last metaphysician'.) Whether or not he is successful, Nietzsche's insistence on style, his persistent, if unsystematic attack on the classical philosophical oppositions – all in the course of doing something closely related to philosophy – is his answer. The product, a philosophy that contests the possibility of philosophy – its own possibility – is what I call a liminal textuality. This particularly applies to his *Twilight of the Idols* and *Thus Spake Zarathustra*. Many of his writings are also what Umberto Eco would call *open* texts in that they solicit, even demand, a high level of reader participation. It is just such participation that Nietzsche so desperately felt the lack of. He who had 'ears behind ears' could not even find others with a single pair pointing in the right direction.

The strengths of a limit text are that as a text at least affiliated to a certain genre – in our case philosophy – its various contestatory moves can be interpreted as questioning philosophy while at the same time never quite destroying it. The limit text allows the writer to explore the margins of a genre by enacting, within a relatively contained space, all sorts of transgressions and dangerous manoeuvres.

But these dangers are rather more obvious in the writing of Derrida. In 1972, Derrida gave a lecture, 'The Question of Style', which was subsequently published in a somewhat different form as *Spurs/Eperons: Nietzsche's Styles*. This too, as it happens, I would call a limit text par excellence.

Properly speaking, we ought to precede any commentary on Derrida's *Spurs* with a discussion of *his* styles, which exceed in complexity anything one finds in Nietzsche. I hope I may be forgiven for citing at this juncture the *OED* entry for that other sort of *stile* (with an *i*), the sort one finds in the country which is defined as 'An arrangement of steps or the like, contrived to allow passage over and through a fence to one person at a time, while forming a barrier to sheep or cattle.' Nietzsche would have liked this: a way through to some, and yet a barrier to others.[8] Was that the real secret of his style? My suspicion is that quite a lot can be learned about *difficult* styles by seeing them as setting up *initiatory thresholds* to prevent *any* understanding below a certain level of active recognition and participation. I admit this description does not entirely apply to Nietzsche. When Heidegger recommended to his students (during a course on Nietzsche!) that they read Aristotle for ten or fifteen years before reading Nietzsche, it was presumably because of the dangerous illusion of his accessibility.

Spurs is a complex interweaving of themes and concerns. Rather than summarize it I will try to catch the drift. Derrida could be said to be concerned with three distinct issues: (1) Nietzsche's apparent anti-feminism. ('Are you visiting women? Do not forget your whip,' the old woman advises Zarathustra in the 'Of Old and Young Women' (*TSZ*)); (2) Heidegger's judgement of Nietzsche as the last metaphysician; (3) the hermeneutic presupposition that in every text there is a decidable meaning (of which Heidegger's willingness to *place* Nietzsche in this way would be an example).

Derrida's strategy is to develop an intimacy between what Nietzsche says about truth, about women and about distance and to use the developed entanglement of these terms, and the subsequent insight as to the role of style in all this, to challenge Heidegger's reading of Nietzsche. A revealing instance will be seen to be Heidegger's passing over in silence the phrase 'truth becomes woman' in Heidegger's otherwise close scrutiny of the passage in *Twilight of the Idols* referred to above. Derrida's aim, though, is *not* to remind us, or Heidegger, of the omnipresence of the question of woman for Nietzsche. Rather he wants to show us that the concept or symbol of 'woman' *for Nietzsche*, is closely bound up with that of *truth*, and has a textual economy subversive of the very ontological framework within which Heidegger is operating when he discusses Nietzsche. Nietzsche's texts, according to Derrida, escape by and large ontological determination, and consequently cannot be described as the last stage of the history of metaphysics. To put it crudely, what appears, superficially, as Nietzsche's style, or styles is, when analysed or explored more fully, a complex post-metaphysical strategy. I will have some critical things to say about Derrida's procedure here, but let me first try to work through this 'argument' a little more slowly.

Under a series of suggestive headings – distances, veils, truths, adornments, simulation – Derrida demonstrates that whatever we may suppose Nietzsche to believe about real women, there is in his various remarks about women what I would in other contexts call an 'underlying logic' or 'deep structure'. Woman functions in

Nietzsche's texts as something like a symbol, and yet the *logic* of that symbol is powerfully unsettling. 'Women are not deep, they are not even shallow,' he remarks at one point. Is he just saying that this pair of terms is inappropriate? He is saying more than that. Women, *to men* (and he says somewhere that men created *woman*) are essentially beings held at a distance, are enchantresses; they *essentially* seem to hold some secret, to be the site of some eternal peace; they are essentially *beautiful, adorned* creatures, tempting us to something beyond appearances. As an example of how *woman* functions in this way, Derrida quotes Nietzsche: 'The world is overfull of beautiful moments, but it is . . . nevertheless poor, very poor, in beautiful things. But perhaps this is the greatest charm of life: it puts a gold-embroidered veil of lovely potentialities over itself, promising, resisting, modest, mocking, sympathetic, seductive. Yes, life is a woman.'9 The parallel between such a concept of woman, which Nietzsche does not suppose himself to have invented, and that of *truth* should be obvious. The history of the philosophical search for truth is that of penetration of the surface, drawing aside the veil of appearances, to what is secret, hidden, covered over.

Now we know that, for Nietzsche, truth is 'an illusion of which we have *forgotten* that *it is* an illusion'. The same can be said of *woman*. And this raises the important question: if we suppose that hidden depth is an illusion, the mere reflection of a desire, should we suppose that what we are left with is mere *appearance* – the world of appearances? One of Heidegger's key criticisms of Nietzsche is, as Derrida points out, that he proceeds very often by inverting Platonic propositions, standing them on their head. Clearly this would not be enough to transcend metaphysical determinations, if Nietzsche was still working within the same oppositional structure. And yet consider: 'Women are considered deep, . . . [they are] not even shallow'10, alongside 'with [the abolition of] the real world we have also abolished the apparent world'11, and recall 'my style is a dance, a play of all kinds of symmetries, and a vaulting and mocking of these symmetries.'12 It is clear that Nietzsche can only be charged with remaining a metaphysician after all on *these* grounds if his overleaping of symmetries had failed. And that means: if his style had not done the work he intended.

Heidegger is not unaware that Nietzsche's strategy is more complex than a reversal and that Nietzsche is as Derrida quotes, 'seeking something else'. For Nietzsche in 'The History of an Error' (*TI*) wants, says Heidegger, to do something not *just* to the terms of the hierarchy (such as inversion) but also to the nature of the hierarchical relation itself. It will be left to Derrida to claim that what Nietzsche is doing is *not* just valuing *appearance* over reality, but diagnosing *the effect of that distance* by which, say, appearance/reality, or the concept of *woman* are constituted.

In Derrida's view, Nietzsche's use of the term *woman* is subversive of ontology. Derrida puts it like this

> There is no such thing as the essence of woman because woman averts, she is averted of herself [*parce que la femme écarte et s'écarte elle-même*]. Out of the depths, endless and unfathomable, she engulfs and distorts all vestige of essentiality, of identity, or property. And philosophical discourse, blinded, founders on these shoals and is hurled down these depthless depths to its ruin. There is no such thing as the truth of woman, but it is because of that abyssal divergence of the truth, because that untruth is 'truth'. Woman is but one name for that untruth of truth.[13]

To cut a longer story shorter, Derrida, having made the question of woman in Nietzsche into a heavily loaded one, can then point to Heidegger's failure to discuss the phrase 'truth becomes woman' in 'The History of an Error' as a symptomatic omission.

Derrida's argument is this: Heidegger's reading of Nietzsche works with the framework of ontology, concerned ultimately with the question of 'the truth of beings'. In a number of different ways, the horizon of ontology is bound up with the concept of *property*, *belonging*, *the proper*, and most importantly for Heidegger, *ereignis* – appropriation. Indeed Heidegger even tries to abandon the notion of being in favour of that of appropriation. Derrida argues that not only is the concept of woman in Nietzsche one that undermines the notion of identity, it also undermines the place of *giving*, within the field of 'property relations'. A woman is a woman in so far as she gives herself *out* to be. (One can think of many other paradoxes of desire and possession.) Derrida's claim is that the concept of *woman*, loaded as we have come to see with questions relating to truth and desire, is a term whose value is *undecidable* in terms of what is proper to or what belongs to her, and as such stands outside that ontological/hermeneutical framework that Heidegger is taking for granted. Nietzsche's writing contains at least the seeds of a critique of the basis on which Heidegger tries to classify it as a metaphysics.

Derrida's version, then, of my less well-developed claim that Nietzsche's writing is a liminal textuality is the claim that Nietzsche's text is marked by a strategy of writing, a style, indeed a multiplicity of styles which does not merely make *its* meaning radically undecidable, but which promotes the cause of undecidability itself, of language *not* subject to metaphysical determination.

Style on this view is absolutely *vital* to Nietzsche's writing. As Derrida puts it: '[T]he reversal, if it is not accompanied by a discrete parody, a strategy of writing, or difference or deviation in quills, if there is no style, this is finally but the same thing, nothing more than a clamorous declaration of the antithesis. Hence the heterogeneity of the text.'14 (The textual economy of woman is just one example. Derrida weaves in an account of *castration* and *truth* as well.)

What then can we make of Derrida's reading in the light of our concern with Nietzsche's styles? (There is more to say about Derrida's reading here – a whole section on umbrellas, for example, which I have not forgotten, but which I will leave unopened.)

It confirms our view of the importance of style in Nietzsche, and his suggestion that it contains ontologically undecidable terms offers a way of filling out the idea of a limit text. There are, however, difficulties with the whole project of harnessing style to achieve otherwise unattainable results. The first is a problem I adapt from a paper of Paul de Man's: if we suppose that Nietzsche's use of style introduces a performative element into the text, why is that any more immune to deconstruction than the original *descriptive* or *referential* dimension? The second problem is with the status of such texts: whether they are merely *reactive*, as Rorty has it.

Consider again Derrida's strategy of reading. He begins with a letter of Nietzsche's, and then, in his first section writes: 'The title for this lecture was to have been the question of style. However – it is woman who will be my subject. Still, one might wonder whether that does not really amount to the same thing – or is it to the other.'15 We have already heard something of what follows. Given the extraordinary wealth of material that Derrida draws together, it may seem bizarre to accuse him of reductionism, but the charge can I believe be sustained. Important as it is, style's ability to repel a metaphysical appropriation of the text is not the only dimension that counts. What Derrida declines is any attempt to deal with what I have called the existential dimension of Nietzsche's style, which I located in Nietzsche's remarks in *Ecce Homo*. Derrida refers to the section, he quotes nine words from it, and passes on to the remarks about women that soon crop up. But he does not mention Nietzsche's account of the multiplicity of his styles as reflections or expressions or embodiments of the plurality of his own physical states.

The reason surely is that while Nietzsche's account here is not one that naively posits a single author or source of his own style, he is committing himself to an *interpretation* of his own stylistic variety in which the frame of reference is expanded beyond the text, and into the body and life of the writer. The dis-ease of the body in each of its states introduces distances of various sorts into the body itself. The text then is a translation of figures that have first a bodily existence, and only then a textual one. It is perhaps no accident that he calls his style a dance. I am not convinced Derrida could happily take all this on board, and yet Nietzsche's use of style is clearly determined by this existential dimension as well as by the semantic, and, if you like, the post-metaphysical dimension.

Let me now turn to my two final questions. First, what I will call de Man's question. It is this: is there not an objection in principle to style being able to *do* something that merely *saying* cannot achieve. Does this not rest on an innocence about action, about *doing* that one would never allow oneself when thinking about describing or referring? The point is this: if style is thought of as an author's way of doing something special in a text, then surely it is open to a deconstructive approach to action, intention and so on, one that can be easily found in Nietzsche himself, when he ridicules the idea of inner causes, the self or ego as origin of action etc. I think this is an objection to giving a privileged status to an author's remarks on what he was trying to do, where this conflicts with what he manifestly did do. And it warns us against thinking of style too much as an externally directly conscious manipulation of language, rather than something in which, as Derrida suggests of Nietzsche, the author may get quite lost, like a spider in his own web. Certainly this raises new questions about Nietzsche's own account of his styles as transformations of his body. The answer might be to attempt to start more explicitly not merely with embodied subjects, but with signifying subjects, which would make the passage from a bodily state to a style less urgently in need of a semiological equivalent of Descartes' pineal gland.

My second question I will call the Rorty question; its broadest version would be: what is the scope and value of such liminal textuality as we find in Nietzsche? Rorty's contribution here is to insist that there is something approaching a tradition of philosophical writing that includes the later Heidegger and the later Wittgenstein too which can be called *reactive*. And Nietzsche is included in this list: 'Great edifying philosophers are reactive and offer satires, parodies, aphorisms. They know their work loses its point when the period they were reacting against is over. They are intentionally peripheral.'[16]

On Rorty's view, it is fatal for a *reactive* philosophy which plays off a tradition that it is deconstructing or attacking or subverting to try to convert itself into a new position, a new system. Nietzsche agrees: 'the will to a system is a lack of integrity'. But if the value of Nietzsche's writing depends on the perpetuation of Platonism, surely it has a rather strange status. If it succeeds in seeing off metaphysics, it eliminates the reason for its existence. If it fails, well it fails. We might suppose that, like the poor, or sin, or starvation, metaphysics is always with us, so that Nietzsche's value is perennial. But this would be precisely to ignore the sense in which Nietzsche claims to have launched through his style a philosophy that is not merely reactive but active and affirmative in a way that transcends the old metaphysical senses of *activity* and *affirmation*. It would be to refuse to join the dance.

This issue is still very much alive today, and here Derrida has inherited the Nietzschean mantle. But the question of whether there can be a single post-metaphysical textuality (or many such textualities) would require a further discussion of the relation between what Heidegger calls *thinking* and what Derrida calls *writing*.

Notes

1 See Heidegger, *Nietzsche*, 4 vols. [1961], trans. D. F. Krell (New York: Harper & Row, 1979–82); and Derrida, *Spurs/Eperons: Nietzsche's Styles* [1978], trans. B. Harlow (Chicago: Chicago University Press, 1979).

2 See W. Kaufmann, *Nietzsche: Philosopher, Psychologist, Antichrist* (New York: Vintage, 1968), esp. Chapter 2.

3 *Ecce Homo*, trans. W. Kaufmann (New York: Vintage, 1969), p. 265 'Why I Write Such Good Books'.

4 Roland Barthes, *Writing Degree Zero* [1953], trans. A. Lavers and C. Smith (London: Cape, 1968), p. 10.

5 *Gay Science*, trans. W. Kaufmann (New York: Vintage, 1975), p. 35.

6 I quote from a translation by Paul de Man in an excellent essay on these notes, his 'Nietzsche's Theory of Rhetoric', *Yale French Studies* (New Haven: Yale University Press, 1974). The original text is in vol. V, *Gesammelte Werke* (Musarion: Munich, 1922).

7 *Beyond Good and Evil*, trans. Helen Zimmern (Edinburgh: Foulis, 1908), Section 20, p. 28.
8 In *Ecce Homo*, p. 197, he writes, 'All the more subtle laws of any style have their origin at this point: they at the same time keep away, create a distance, forbid 'entrance' ... '
9 *Spurs*, pp. 51–3.
10 *Twilight of the Idols*, trans. R. J. Hollingdale (Harmondsworth: Penguin, 1968), p. 25.
11 ibid., p. 41.
12 'Letter to Rohde' [1884], in *Selected Letters*, trans. A. N. Ludovici (London: Soho Books, 1985), p. 173.
13 *Spurs*, p. 51.
14 ibid., p. 95.
15 ibid., pp. 35–7.
16 *Philosophy and the Mirror of Nature* (Oxford: Blackwell, 1980), p. 369. There is a certain insensitivity in using the term 'reactive' here, given Nietzsche's own valuation of the active over the reactive. Deleuze makes much of this distinction.

Further reading

Nietzsche's own writings are of course the most important reading here. The well-known essay 'Truth and Falsity in Their Ultramoral Sense' offers an early and extreme statement of his views on language, while books like *Ecce Homo* and *Thus Spake Zarathustra* are most interesting from the point of view of style. The importance of Nietzsche for considering the limits of philosophy is best seen, perhaps, in *Twilight of the Idols*, especially 'How the Real World at Last Became a Myth', in *Beyond Good and Evil*, Section 20, and in the various accounts of the doctrine of eternal recurrence (in *Thus Spake Zarathustra*, and *The Will to Power*). The significance of the various styles and levels of presentation of the doctrine of eternal recurrence, which chafes at the limits of intelligibility, is discussed at length in 'Nietzsche's Transvaluation of Time', Part One of my *The Deconstruction of Time* (Atlantic Highlands: Humanities Press, 1989).

It will be apparent that my sympathies lie more with the French Nietzscheans of the 1970s (in which I include Deleuze, Lyotard, Klossowski, Kofman) and with Derrida, than with the common Anglo-American judgements that would make him a kind of analytic philosopher (see A. Danto, *Nietzsche as Philosopher* [London: Macmillan, 1965]) or would make him into a man of letters. A fine example of the latter is Erich Heller's *The Importance of Nietzsche* (Chicago: Chicago University Press, 1988). An excellent source book of the 'French' reading of Nietzsche is D. Allison (ed.), *The New Nietzsche* (Delta, 1977). Inspired by such sources: an excellent collection *Why Nietzsche Now?* (*Boundary 2*, vol. IX, no. 3 and vol. X, no. 1), and D. F. Krell and D. C. Wood (eds), *Exceedingly Nietzsche* (London: Routledge, 1988). One of the seminal works of that period, Gilles Deleuze's *Nietzsche and Philosophy*, was published in

English by the Athlone Press in 1983. The most accessible, though not very sympathetic, overview of French Nietzscheanism is Vincent Descombes's *Modern French Philosophy* (Cambridge: Cambridge University Press, 1979).

But the central debate about Nietzsche and style within continental philosophy centres around Heidegger's two-volume study (four volumes in English), *Nietzsche*, trans. D. F. Krell (New York: Harper & Row, 1979–82), to which Derrida's *Spurs/Eperons: Nietzsche's Styles* (Chicago, 1979) is something of a reply. Heidegger's verdict on Nietzsche hangs on what one makes of his 'style(s)'. Derrida returns (with others) to Nietzsche in *The Ear of the Other: Otobiography, Transference, Translation* [1982] (New York, Schoeken, 1986).

6

Indirect communication

The history of philosophy has seen the rise and fall of many different attitudes to what we might tentatively call ordinary language. It has been embraced as a mine of useful distinctions and a fountain of common sense (Austin). It has been taken as one of the many subject-matters of philosophy (in the philosophy of language). It has been abandoned in despair at its vagueness, its looseness, its unsuitability for rigorous thought, in favour of logically reconstructed languages, such as were proposed by Carnap and Russell. It has been supplemented by technical terms, and it has had its intrinsic lexical and syntactic productivity exploited by Hegel and Heidegger. Each of these ways of endorsing, improving or transforming ordinary language is interesting in its own right, but I would like here to consider a somewhat different project for the transformation of language. Broadly speaking we could call it a change of style.

There are two distinct reasons for supposing that the philosophical inadequacies of language can be corrected by a change of style, depending on where one thinks the main inadequacy lies. There is the belief in ordinary language's semantic inadequacy, and the belief in its existential inadequacy. I associate the first particularly with Nietzsche and the second with Kierkegaard.

On the first view, we need a change of style (for philosophical purposes) to overcome the illusoriness of language as such. The same words are applied to different objects, falsely suggesting that discrete objects can be qualitatively identical when observation tells us there is no identity in the world, only differences.

On the second view, a change of style is needed to handle particular problems of linguistic expression – those associated with the expression of inwardness or subjectivity, as Kierkegaard put it.

Each of these views addresses the philosophical inadequacy of ordinary language (or, better, the naive representational way in which language is ordinarily understood). The semantic inadequacy of the belief that the structure of the world is reflected in our language may be harmless enough in everyday life, but it is fatal to philosophy. Nietzsche's claim is that all words are in some sense metaphors, that literal truths are not possible, and that the best way of ensuring that we do not forget this is by exploiting a profusion of semantic, syntactic and rhetorical devices which wear their non-representativeness and non-seriousness on their sleeves.

The correction of existential inadequacy follows a different route. It does not specially involve lexical changes, nor syntactic changes (as with Hegel), though Kierkegaard's language is often quite as dialectical as Hegel's. Principally, it involves, on those particular occasions when it is philosophically called for, a change in one's mode of communication. What inwardness requires, says Kierkegaard, is indirect communication.

Kierkegaard's philosophical position can best be grasped as a positive reaction against Hegel's (as well as to institutionalized Christian theology). In particular as we have suggested, Kierkegaard was outraged at the conceit and self-delusion (as he saw it) of the Hegelian system. This grand synthesis aimed at offering a total rational description of man, society, history and nature as the development of spirit to complete self-consciousness. To provide this project with such key terms as consciousness, self-consciousness, subject, spirit, etc. Hegel had to steal them from the point of their obvious application to individuals, and use them to construct a system so fantastic that it denies the significance of individuals, and their particular subjectivity. For Hegel, there is only the bloodless category of individuality, but there are no actual individuals. Hegel, said Kierkegaard, cannot deal with the actual, with the existent, without transforming it into a concept or a notion.

Hegel's whole philosophical system involves taking up the attitude of philosophical and historical detachment, a position from which individual subjective existence – the dramas of commitment, decision, responsibility, belief, etc. – is invisible. It can be assimilated but not appreciated. And finally, says Kierkegaard, Hegel is blind to his own existence. He cannot live in the castle he has built; he rather lives in a hut next door. The system is an existential fraud.

In opposition to Hegel, Kierkegaard develops an account of individuality from the point of view of the thinker who reflects on his existence from within. Whereas stones and stools can perhaps be subsumed under categories without significant loss, this is not the case with existing individuals, who not only derive the significance of their actions from the categories into which they objectively fall, but also give meaning to themselves.

Kierkegaard's whole mission is to rescue inwardness, or subjectivity from under the boot of Hegelian universalism.

Hegel's philosophical absorption of individuality into the system – according to which only what is systematic is true – has its practical parallel in the threat posed by social conventions and norms to individuality, especially to an individual acutely aware of himself as 'an exception'.

Clearly, for Kierkegaard, subjective existence is no mere aspect of philosophy but the basis on which philosophical problems matter at all, even if it does not in itself provide all the answers. So the existential inadequacy of language, as we have called it, is a serious matter.

It might be objected here that Kierkegaard's problems with Hegel are no longer our problems, that Hegel is no longer the dominant force in philosophy that he once was. Quite the reverse is true. There are very few contemporary continental philosophers on whom Hegel has not made a major impact; there is a lively and accelerating scholarly interest in Hegel today, discovering a Hegel much more congenial to Kierkegaard; and Kierkegaard's relation to Hegel finds intriguing echoes in the relationship between the French philosopher Emmanuel Levinas and the work of Heidegger.[1] Moreover, the general form of Kierkegaard's position could be articulated equally well against certain forms of Marxism, sociologism, and indeed any form of reductionism for which the individual is a mere 'unit'.

It might still be objected that subjectivity is not worthy of his (or our) philosophical concern, associated as it is with partiality, and with error (in being opposed, for example, to objectivity). Is not subjectivity always 'mere', a deficient attitude? Is it not always idiosyncratic, unreliable, a haven for the personal, the psychological – perhaps fascinating material for journalists but not for philosophy? The proper reply to all this is that much of what we call 'objective' is dependent on the cognitive (and other) capacities of 'subjects' and in this sense on the subjective; that there is nothing necessarily misleading or inferior about subjectivity. One can study conscious activity philosophically and even, dare one say it, objectively (what else is phenomenology all about?), and show that what we call the error or one-sidedness of subjectivity is often actually a positive, constitutive feature of what it is to be an individual – having to take up positions without compelling evidence.

When Kierkegaard turns the table, and says that subjectivity is truth what he means is that the essence of being human is one's 'ethical' existence, one's commitments, one's relation to limit-situations, and so on. The assessment of subjectivity as error mistakenly applies epistemological standards to existence. One's ethical life is real, and so much the worse for an account of what there is that excludes or relegates it.

We can now see why indirect communication might be of some value. But why does Kierkegaard believe that only indirect communication can capture the subjective? Surely we can express the subjective quite directly. Is not pain subjective? And can we not say 'I am in pain' quite directly? If I tell you of my feelings of pleasure at being able to talk to you, is that not a direct statement of the subjective?

The simple answer is no, not in Kierkegaard's sense of subjectivity. Or rather they are examples of what we could call immediate subjectivity, whereas Kierkegaard is concerned with a form of subjectivity which is reflected. We can only understand why indirect communication is necessary if we understand what he means by this reflected form of subjectivity. His account is developed in the section of *Concluding Unscientific Postscript* entitled 'The Subjective Existing Thinker Has Regard to the Dialectics of the Process of Communication'.

The argument has three stages. It begins with the claim that there are essentially two types of thought and therefore thinkers: objective and subjective. Kierkegaard expands on this distinction as follows: objective thought abstracts from 'the thinking subject and his existence'. It 'translates everything into results' and 'helps all mankind to cheat, by copying these off and reciting them by rote'. The subjective thinker on the other hand 'is an existing individual essentially interested in his own thinking, existing as he does in his thought'. He is involved in the process of his thought, and less in its results. After all, he is constantly becoming, not an objective thing.

It is worth noting that Kierkegaard writes as if objective thought was not actually performed by anyone. This impression will later recede.

The second stage of the argument is to claim that in this distinction between objective and subjective thinking we can detect a difference between the kind of reflection involved in each. Objective thought involves reflection, but subjective thinking involves a double reflection.

What he means is this: in both cases, thinking involves thinking about something, which Kierkegaard calls the universal. Minimally this means that thinking involves subsuming things under categories, recognizing universality or meaning in particular things, occasions, situations. Reflection goes beyond what is merely given, and takes it up at the level of concepts. So far both types of thinking are the same. But subjective thinking involves a second stage of reflection. This he calls 'a reflection of inwardness, of possession, by virtue of which it belongs to the thinking subject and to no one else'. That is, the subjective thinker is significantly aware that it is he who is thinking his thoughts, and presumably of what they mean for him in his particular state of existence. The idea is at least this: that for the subjective thinker thinking is an activity, one that fully engages him, not merely something going on inside him, like a tape cassette playing in his head. And this engagement, the way his thinking matters for his life, will be part of the structure and process of that thought itself, and not just an external attitude to it.

The last stage of the argument is the claim that we can make a distinction between direct and indirect communication, and that only indirect communication is capable of handling this doubly reflected, subjective thinking. Kierkegaard's argument is to be found in a foot-note.[2] There is a contradiction between the inwardness of subjective thinking, and the outwardness of direct public expression. 'This contradiction,' says Kierkegaard, 'cannot possibly find expression in a direct form'.

To see that there is a contradiction we have to remember that by 'inwardness' he means that my thinking is both an activity (not adequately reflected in a summary of results) and something that intimately concerns me (and as such cannot just be said).

Direct communication, which just repeats the thoughts in question, is inadequate both because it has to leave out this second set of considerations and because it pretends it has not left anything out.

Kierkegaard gives the following example:

A lover, for example, whose inwardness is his love, may very well wish to communicate but he will not wish to communicate himself directly, precisely because the inwardness of his love is for him essential. Essentially occupied constantly in acquiring and reacquiring the inwardness of love, he has no result, and is never finished. But he may . . . still want to communicate although he can never use a direct form, because such a form presupposes results and finality. (*CUP*, p. 68)

Kierkegaard is returning here to the activity argument – that because individuals are in active process, a communicative mode that interrupted this flow with a verdict, a judgement, would be false. He similarly argues that direct communication 'presupposes certainty'; but as we are always in a process of becoming, we cannot have certainty.

On the face of it this claim about certainty seems plainly false. If I say, quite directly, 'I believe that . . . ' I am not committed to certainty. What he means however is that what he wants to express is not a fact about himself, nor a state, but a striving, plagued with doubt, the risk of failure, the need for constant reaffirmation and so on. He could indeed spell all that out, but that would not be an expression of love, but a description of its inner trials. And to express his love would be to transform this state of flux into an assured attitude and indeed make a commitment, and Kierkegaard is clearly thinking of a love that is too unstable to be relied on in that way.

The example of love is not the only one Kierkegaard uses. The problem of the religious man's expression of his relation with God and of the reasons for his actions which follow from that relation (the problems of faith and paradox) are expressed clearly in his account of the Abraham story in *Fear and Trembling*.

According to Kierkegaard, then, there are two kinds of reflection, objective and subjective. To understand how indirect communication is possible we must grasp what it is about ordinary communication that is being changed.

Kierkegaard says at one point that 'The objective accent falls on *what* is said, the subjective accent on *how* it is said' (*CUP*, p. 181). Clearly subjective reflection has to work on the *how* side of communication. And we can see how the distinction between objective and subjective reflection can be cashed out in speech or writing in terms of a distinction between syntactic reflexivity on the one hand, and enactment on the other. By syntactic reflexivity, I mean simply a sentence taking a sentence as its subject ('It is a shame that P'). P is being reflected upon objectively. Kierkegaard himself describes the alternative – what I have called *enactment* – in the following terms: '[T]his form should embody artistically as much of reflection as he himself has when existing in his thought. In an artistic manner, please note; for the secret does not lie in a direct assertion of the double reflection' (*CUP*, p. 68).

So, in a form like irony, the art lies not in constructing a reflective syntax, but in a certain allusiveness captured by one's words. There is a parallel between Kierkegaard's enactment here, a performance which points to the subjectivity which enlivens it, and the way the later Heidegger allows language to show itself.[3] But clearly there is something missing from this account. After all, Kierkegaard is talking about indirect communication and not just indirect expression. This is important both because no adequate account of language can forget its communicative role, and for the special reason that it is communication that poses the problem for Kierkegaard. One is immediately aware of one's own subjective life, but ordinary language seems to give it voice only at the cost of betraying it. So Kierkegaard must say something about communication.

Some might think that it is exactly here that we will discover the fundamental error of Kierkegaard's account, that in some way or other his position can be subjected to Wittgenstein's arguments against private languages.

Wittgenstein argued that there is and could be no way of conceptually ordering one's private experience that would not involve applying rules by which the elements of that experience could be repeatedly recognized. To fail to employ such rules would mean that there would cease to be a distinction between having a certain experience again and having an experience that one thought was the same. Sameness has no sense without rules of identity and thus of re-identification. And if one does employ such tacit rules, they can be learned and employed by others, at least in principle. For rules are essentially public. One can use private codes, or private criteria for naming and recognizing experiences, but they could only ever be empirically private, not private in principle.

We might suppose that Kierkegaard is falling into the error of positing the logical privacy of inwardness by insisting that it cannot be directly expressed. For it seems to imply that inwardness or subjectivity can take this or that form, that it can have a particular character, without being able to be captured by ordinary direct language. And surely to have one particular character rather than another is to fall under this rule for identification rather than that. So surely public language – perhaps lexically extended – is good enough.

There are three replies to this: firstly, Kierkegaard would, I think, reject this last argument. He would deny that inwardness needs to have a particular objective feature in the way suggested. That it is mine, for example (which of course is true for everyone), does not distinguish it qualitatively or conceptually, but it does distinguish it existentially.

There is a difference for me (and indeed for him) between my being faced with an agonizing decision, and someone else being faced with the same decision, a difference which is not captured by saying that David Wood and Mr X are distinct individuals.

The second reply to the Wittgensteinian objection is that Wittgenstein himself did not make the extreme claim that all subjectivity was directly expressible, and even refers to Kierkegaard in talking about the limits of language. Consider such remarks as:

> Nevertheless we do run up against the limits of language. This running up against Kierkegaard also recognised and even designated it in a quite similar way (as running up against Paradox). This running up against the limits of language is Ethics. (Here) Everything which we feel like saying can, *a priori*, only be nonsense . . . Yet the tendency represented by the running up against points to something.[4]

The third reply to this general objection is that of course Kierkegaard is not denying that inwardness can be expressed in a public language. What he is insisting on is that one adopt a particular way of using this language to get it across, a language that points. So Kierkegaard would agree with Wittgenstein that such language was unable to express inwardness directly, but add that indirect language could do this.

We are now in a position to discuss what has so far been lacking – the specifically communicative aspect of indirect communication.

Communication of whatever sort involves not just a speaker but a hearer too. Kierkegaard seems to be saying that the distinction is between direct communication, in which A says something to B and B understands the immediate literal meaning of what he says, and indirect communication, in which A says something and B understands not merely what his words mean but A's point in uttering those words, where this point conveys (in irony, say) a certain distance from the direct semantic content, in which distance inwardness can be indicated. In indirect communication, one's words indirectly convey something other than their direct meaning, which is subjectivity.

The distinction Kierkegaard is using here, as we have described it, seems to be importantly underpinned by the kind of account of speech acts offered by Austin, and developed by Searle and in Grice's 'logic of conversation'. A brief outline of this theory will also help us with a very puzzling claim which we will shortly encounter.

112

Austin began with a distinction between locutionary, illocutionary and perlocutionary speech acts. Locutionary acts are simply utterances; illocutionary acts are linguistic acts in which one can be said to do something – like stating, denying or asking; perlocutionary acts are acts in which one aims at producing certain effects by one's words, such as getting someone to do something.

Searle's position involves among other things the elimination of locutionary acts as independent entities, treating the fact of utterance as a necessary condition of an illocutionary act. The general picture offered by the speech-act theory is that speech is the primary form of communication, that such communication consists of speech acts, that all speech acts have both propositional content, an intentional backing and make use of conventions.

We are now in a position to understand what would otherwise be a rather difficult remark: that direct communication is not really a form of communication at all. There are two initial ways of understanding this claim: that all communication strictly speaking is indirect, and that only indirect communication realizes some ideal of communication. The first alternative is one for which Searle oddly enough can be seen as offering reasons. Thus, he explains the role of intention in speech acts in the following way: 'In speaking a language I attempt to communicate things to my hearer by means of getting him to recognise my intention to communicate just those things.'[5]

On this acount, it would seem that all communication is in a sense indirect. What we produce are sounds, or words, or at most sentences under certain conditions. These are the direct content of communication. But what makes it possible to understand them is understanding what the author was using these words to say, or do; what he or she meant by them.

What we need is a distinction between two senses of indirect communication. In the first broad sense, it is an aspect of most if not all communication that one grasps the point of what someone is saying by means of the words used. But Kierkegaard's idea of indirect communication seems rather narrower that this, and to involve a specification of a range of intentions that are to be carried. Kierkegaard opts for the second alternative – that only indirect communication realizes some communicative ideal. One's communicative acts point not merely to an intention, but to the subjectivity of the being that intends. Indirect communication has an ontological status not merely a psychological one.

Arguably, then, in this narrow ontological sense, we are dealing with a subset of perlocutionary acts, with acts which bring about an effect other than the recognition of an intention. The effect intended by existential irony, for example, is the recognition of the impossibility of the direct expression of the speaker's inwardness or subjectivity. And in principle this could be brought about by other means such as a gesture.

Clearly, on this account, what is important is not just the double reflection performed by the speaker but also the process of understanding undergone by the hearer, a process that Austin called uptake.

It is at this point that Kierkegaard's whole account of indirect communication seems to spring to life. So far we have been concerned with the problems of expression, of running up against the limits of direct language. The problem is one faced by each individual for himself and herself. Kierkegaard adds, however, an important twist to the story when he describes the hearer's uptake. For true communication, that is, indirect communication, involves the emancipation of the listener or reader. To understand a particular statement, one has to go through the same moves as the speaker went through in producing his words. And in going through these moves one acquaints oneself not just with the speaker but with one's own inwardness. And one is thereby emancipated from self-objectification. In this respect we must clearly count indirect communication as a perlocutionary act – an existential perlocution.

With this theme of emancipation, we are shot forward to the twentieth century. Kierkegaard's influence here can be felt particularly in the work of the Frankfurt school (especially Adorno) and in Heidegger's account of authentic solicitude. The powerful implication of Kierkegaard's account here is that, in a sense not often noticed, communication has an important ethical dimension. And this explains why Kierkegaard is not just making the Searlean claim that in a sense all communication is indirect. Kierkegaard's claim is stronger than this: that communication is primarily an intersubjective relationship, and does not take place unless the speaker or both speaker and hearer reveal themselves as existing subjects in his strong sense. Or, to put it another way, true communication is an ontological, not a psychological affair.

So far I have tried to show how Kierkegaard developed his account of indirect communication, and what purpose it was designed to serve.

I have tried to present the account in as plausible a light as possible. But I would like to conclude with a few questions, critical pointers to further discussion.

What is the philosophical scope of this doctrine? Kierkegaard might be claiming that philosophical discourse must take the indirect form, or that an adequate philosophy of language must take indirect communication into account; or, finally, that especially important parts of philosophy require the indirect form of discourse. I think the last position is the one he would opt for. As he sees it, philosophical issues are fundamentally existential. That is to say that finally philosophical questions are questions that concern us existentially and not merely cognitively, and that this concern is constitutive of them as philosophical questions. He cannot suppose that the objective form of thought is without value; rather it is fundamentally at the service of the subjective. And indirect communication is the only proper expression of that subjectivity. So Kierkegaard sees indirect communication as fundamental but not necessary or general. He can allow ordinary philosophy to continue, but would add that it only comes into its own when its existential significance is drawn out.

More critically, how are we to judge the aim of indirect communication, which seems to be something like existential community, a communion of souls? It goes beyond, we have suggested, a shared understanding of the meaning of the meaning of a particular speech act. It involves a grasp of the subjective presence of the other. Is not Kierkegaard appealing to the arch-metaphysical concept of presence here? Is this idealized inter-subjectivity not as suspect as the idea of immediate self-knowledge, of immediate perception? Is it not an attempt more specifically to paper over the differences that divide us from one another, as well as within ourselves? Is not what Kierkegaard is describing a fantasy, a desire for the presence of the other, or presence to the other? Is not Kierkegaard under the illusion that he can gain by a magical formula – indirect communication – what he cannot gain directly? I do not think so. For Kierkegaard, indirect communication has two different effects: it allows the other to grasp that one is an existing being struggling, at this point, with the limits of language, without necessitating intimate insight into what that inwardness might consist of. And it allows the other to grasp or reawaken his own inwardness as a field to explore – the emancipatory content of indirect communication. But neither of these effects involves the pure presence that a Derridean might have anticipated. The grasp by the other of one's inwardness is not the same as – is necessarily different from – one's own acquaintance with it. And the emancipatory effects of indirect communication in no way involve a communion. It may be that in the moment at which we see the dawning of the smile of understanding on the face of the other that we are the closest we can get to true community – a nexus of interintentional recognition – but we must not pretend that it is pure, or simple. Nor need we idealize it.

The main conclusion of this chapter could be summed up as follows: that there may be limits to what we can communicate which are specific to a particular mode of communication, and can be overcome by a change of style. The very non-propositional nature of existential inwardness that direct communication finds it so hard to put across is what makes it possible to communicate it indirectly – not as a *what*, but as a way. While this result is important, it is not one that should alarm those for whom direct communication is a way of life. It is a special kind of perlocutionary act, with a limited though privileged field of application. And I can only think that A. J. Ayer was endorsing the work of Nietzsche and Kierkegaard when he wrote: 'the fact that in all philosophy so much depends on the way things are put gives point to the saying that philosophy is an exercise in rhetoric'.

In the next chapter I discuss a particular case of the problem of communication, one in which the relation to the other is reflexively tied up with philosophical views about that very possibility – the 'encounter' between Derrida and Gadamer.

Notes

1 See Emmanuel Levinas' *Existence and Existents*, trans. A Lingis (The Hague: Nijhoff, 1978); and *Totality and Infinity*, trans. A Lingis (Pittsburgh: Duquesne University Press, 1969), esp. Section I, A. See also Robert Bernasconi and David Wood (eds), *The Provocation of Levinas: Rethinking the Other* (London: Routledge, 1988), and Sean Hand (ed.), *The Levinas Reader* (Oxford: Blackwell, 1989). For our purposes what is most important is Levinas's distinction between *le dire* and *le dit*, saying and the said. The face-to-face relation inhabits the (infinite) realm of saying. See especially his *Otherwise than Being or Beyond Essence*, trans. A. Lingis (The Hague: Nijhoff, 1981).
2 *Concluding Unscientific Postscript* (*CUP*) [1846] (Princeton: Princeton University Press, 1941), p. 68.
3 See my *The Deconstruction of Time* (Atlantic Highlands: Humanities Press, 1989), Part 4, Chapter 3.

4   From 'Zu Heidegger', in Chapter 6 of Michael Murray (ed.), *Heidegger and Modern Philosophy* (New Haven: Yale, 1978).
5   Searle, 'What Is a Speech Act?' (1965), in John Searle (ed.), *The Philosophy of Language* (Oxford: Oxford University Press, 1971), pp. 39–53.

Further reading

The reader of Kierkegaard's *Concluding Unscientific Postscript* (Princeton: Princeton University Press, 1941) should not miss the Appendix in which Kierkegaard confesses all his pseudonyms. The *need* for indirectness, for rhetorical masks, in order for philosophy to communicate, is one Kierkegaard explores further in *The Concept of Irony* (Bloomington: Indiana University Press, 1968); the pragmatics of silence are explored in *Fear and Trembling* (Princeton: Princeton University Press, 1941); and an excellent collection of critical essays on Kierkegaard – including 'The Master of Irony' by the editor, Josiah Thompson – can be found in *Kierkegaard* (New York: Anchor, 1972).

The theory of speech acts is best pursued through Austin's *How to Do Things with Words* (Oxford: Clarendon Press, 1962), Searle's *Speech Acts*, and through Paul Grice's work on conversation. The most celebrated debate involving deconstruction and speech-act theory is found in the two volumes of *Glyph* (1977) in papers by Derrida and Searle. What is at stake is the relative status of speech and *writing*, in Derrida's new sense.

Through his concern for an *emancipatory* discourse and his diagnosis of the limits of a merely declarative discourse, Kierkegaard had a considerable impact on some members of the Frankfurt school, notably Adorno, who wrote a major study on Kierkegaard's aesthetics in 1933, but also Habermas. Kierkegaard's focus on an ideal mode of communication as the locus for emancipation is shared, despite major differences, by Habermas, who develops the idea of an 'emancipatory interest'. Habermas's most important work on communication is his 'What Is Universal Pragmatics?', in *Communication and the Evolution of Society* (Boston: Beacon Press, 1979). On Adorno, see Gillian Rose's *The Melancholy Science: An Introduction to the Thought of Theodor W. Adorno* (London: Macmillan, 1978). An important book on Kierkegaard by Gillian Rose, *The Broken Middle: Our Ancient Society* (Oxford: Blackwell), is forthcoming.

7

Vigilance and interruption: Derrida, Gadamer and the limits of dialogue

An early theme of Conan Doyle's Sherlock Holmes story *The Hound of the Baskervilles* was *the dog that didn't bark in the night*. My concern too is with something that did not happen. It did not happen when it could well have happened, in 1981, and it has not happened since: a debate, a confrontation between Derrida and Gadamer.

Why might this be philosophically important? Because Derrida and Gadamer are the most important representatives of deconstruction and hermeneutics respectively, which are often seen to occupy opposite poles within continental philosophy. Deconstruction is said to be concerned with the detailed dismantling of the integrity and unity of philosophical and literary texts, and suspicious of every trace of 'presence', of fixation of meaning, of points of secure understanding; while hermeneutics is committed to interpretation, to understanding texts, to a reading which deepens meaning rather than breaking it up, and aims at completeness of understanding. It is not hard to see hermeneutics as radical with regard to a kind of methodological scientism, but as highly conservative compared to the apparently more anarchic tendencies of deconstruction.

An encounter between Gadamer and Derrida might be thought to be as important an event within continental philosophy as the debate between Habermas and Lyotard on post-modernism, or between Derrida and Searle. It might have made clearer what is involved in making a choice between deconstruction and hermeneutics. And whatever background interests one would bring to this debate, its significance is not restricted to issues within the philosophy of language, but has enormous impact on the possibilities of human relation, the ethics of communication and the ideal of human community.

And of course *something* did happen in 1981,[1] which has been described as a meeting of the deaf – a problem of ears, we might say – and since then many people have made strenuous efforts to make that non-event into the seed of a real one.[2] And the theoretical, ethical and eventually political questions we broach are raised not just through the two positions (deconstruction/hermeneutics) put into debate, but in the very fact that that debate seems to have been wilfully refused. I will pursue these questions at both levels.

I shall try to show that much of Derrida's position can be stated in Gadamer's own terms. In doing so, I aim to raise the stakes of the debate: perhaps Derrida has simply failed to take Gadamer seriously. Then I explain the serious motives behind Derrida's apparently perverse refusal to engage Gadamer in true dialogue or open debate. After this I offer some more sophisticated answers to various of these questions than were previously possible, and I argue for a renewed vigilance over the practical implementation of the philosophical ideal of community.

What did happen in 1981? Gadamer read a paper in Paris called 'Text and interpretation', to which, overnight, and (apparently) not feeling quite himself, Derrida wrote a short reply, posing three questions. Since then, Derrida has added nothing, except a tangential essay on Nietzsche, 'Interpreting signatures', which indirectly bears on the difference between his critical assessment of Heidegger's *Nietzsche*, and Gadamer's more positive assessment. Gadamer, on the other hand, has written profusely. The one thing Gadamer and Derrida agree on is that they doubt whether a serious encounter took place. But given that Derrida has clearly had the opportunity since, and has not taken it, we might ask whether his uncharacteristically short and indeed inadequate reply was not carefully attuned to the situation.

Gadamer's 'Text and interpretation' paper has offered an account of texts as, to use his own words, 'a phase in the event of understanding'. The main difference between the spoken and the written word is that the horizons of interpretation which can be gathered by the give and take of conversation have to be supplied within a written text. Gadamer offers an account of textuality, in general, one that treats as residual and exceptional those texts, such as ideological or psychoanalytical

119

texts, for which one would need what Ricoeur called a hermeneutics of suspicion.[3]

Gadamer's account of textuality here involves substantial analogies between reading and writing on the one hand and dialogue on the other. In each case, there is a drive to understanding which, when it occurs, involves a 'fusion of horizons'. Gadamer is offering an account of language as a necessary mediation between human beings.

Derrida's response was to pose questions about two topics: the good will, and the completeness of understanding.

First, when Gadamer says that by entering into dialogue we must have the good will to try to understand each other, is this not an idea affiliated to Kant's idea of the good will, and is that not subject to the problems attached to the idea of will as a metaphysical notion linked to subjectivity and domination? Is not this apparently neutral condition, in other words, already loaded?

Second, Derrida doubts whether we do (as Gadamer suggests) ever have the experience of 'completely understanding the other's meaning'. Is there not a necessary moment of distance, *interruption*, as he expresses it, in all such mediation?

I will focus initially on the question of the limits of understanding. There are two difficulties with Derrida's response to this. It is clearly incomplete in that it does not consider Gadamer's own developed and subtle views on understanding and the limits of understanding. Moreover these remarks are in no way an adequate response to a text, even in Derrida's terms. And, as Gadamer himself argues, Derrida's response constitutes a performative self-contradiction. For surely he must want to be understood!

What would an adequate response look like? A minimal requirement for an adequate reading of a text, response to a paper, and perhaps even listening to another, involves, if only as a first step, an attempt to reconstitute the space of questions and problems within which it is written, spoken or thought. And if *any* sort of analogical projection from self to other is justified, it is the one which treats the other not as some simple self-same identity, nor even as a process, but as engaged in a struggle. This idea is common to a number of thinkers. I will not at this point choose a version of this story.

In Gadamer's case there is surely a struggle, or at the very least a tension, between teleological closure (aiming at a complete understanding) and a necessary openness, exposure and risk. Derrida's failure is to have focused only on the aspect of closure. So I will try to fill out this conflict a little more fully by restoring the other party to the struggle.

Gadamer makes many remarks about the limits to understanding, and the significance of what Wittgenstein would call 'running up against those limits'.

In his response to Derrida's response to him, and after a passage of masterly irony, Gadamer writes: 'I would not want to say that the solidarities which bind human beings together and make them partners in a dialogue always are sufficient to enable them to achieve understanding and total mutual agreement.'[4] This is an important claim, but it remains at the level of there being special exceptions. The norm is unaffected. Derrida's repeated move is to claim that what is thought of as a feature of the exceptional case is constitutive of the normal. Gadamer's entire sensitive analytical distinction between different types of texts, giving the literary text a special treatment, would be subject to such a demarginalizing reversal. But Gadamer's next two remarks are of a different order: 'Just between two people this [understanding and total mutual agreement] would require a never-ending dialogue. And the same would apply with regard to the inner dialogue the soul has with itself.'[5]

What this suggests is that dialogues based on non-topic-based relationships, such as friendship, cannot be dealt with by reference to such a fusion of horizons.[6] For we seem at the very least to be dealing with a horizon of horizons, or even an inexhaustibility of horizons. Does not Gadamer here make room for a space – perhaps even an ethical space – beyond the hermeneutics of understanding, a space akin to what allows Derrida's reference to the *otherness of the other?*

Dialogue never ends not for lack of time or opportunity but for essential reasons. The other resists complete understanding not just because his or her own inner dialogue makes him or her a changing target (as would be the case for Kierkegaard), but because life, if we can use that term, cannot be summed up as a collection of horizons. That Gadamer is explicitly committed to this position is also suggested by his claim (about dialogue) that

> there is something else in this experience, namely a potentiality for being other that lies beyond every coming to agreement about what is common. This is the limit that Hegel did not transgress.[7]

121

Or again

> My own efforts were directed toward not forgetting the limit that is implicit in every hermeneutical experience of meaning. When I wrote the sentence 'Being which can be understood is language', what was implied thereby was that that which is can never be completely understood.[8]

This suggests that whatever thematized relation I may have to another (for example, in trying to understand what he is saying), another relation is always possible – one in which I recognize that to understand that other fully would take a lifetime. If this is true of the other for essential reasons, then we have opened up an ethical space in the midst of thematizing dialogue. If the other is grasped as resistant to any finite understanding then we have surely grasped the otherness of the other. If this is so then we have found in Gadamer an analogue to that insistence on alterity that Derrida seemed to find lacking. This has been achieved by exploiting what could be called a tension in Gadamer's thought, between the analysis of understanding as an event that takes place at the point of fusion of horizons, or as a process that presupposes the possibility of such finite convergence, on the one hand, and the recognition that non-thematized relationships involve, in a positive not privative sense, a never-ending dialogue in which fusion, we might say, is forever deferred. This moment of distance is in some sense always recoverable even at the moment of understanding, even at the moment at which I understand what you are saying quite as clearly as if I had caught a ball you had thrown to me. Derrida's version of this adds that this moment is essential for any relation to be a relation to the other *qua* other.

Derrida queried Gadamer's reference to 'that experience we all recognize, of knowing in a dialogue that one has been understood perfectly'. If Gadamer is right, and I am sure he is, we have also all had the experience of having had our confidence in having been understood perfectly shattered by a development in the dialogue, or by a subsequent turn of events. And however unlikely particular circumstances make this, it is surely always *possible*. One can explain this possibility with fairly minimal premises, such as semantic indeterminacy. But if we start to consider the link between understanding and application,[9] and the inability to predict difficulties in application from an original understanding, and if we add all the difficulties associated with unstated counter-factual conditions, questions about the force of the remarks in question, it seems too easy to construct the case for the necessary possibility of being misunderstood. One only has to think of contracts and promises in which the most careful draughtsmanship seems powerless to anticipate all eventualities.

We do have what might be called stronger experiences of communicative success, in which we are not only sure in some non-reflexive sense that we have been understood perfectly but actually thematize the complexity of this judgement, and still affirm it. But no such multiplication of levels of assurance can outflank the possibilities we mentioned before.

Taking courage and direction from Gadamer's frequent references to the risk and exposure involved in dialogue, never quite knowing what to expect, I would like at this point to suggest another possible consequence of Gadamer's reference to never-ending dialogue with others, as indeed with oneself.

Gadamer claims that understanding is a projective activity and that we can think of that projectivity in terms of an openness he calls a *horizon*. If, however, any particular act or process of understanding occurs within the ongoing life of the subject, surely any particular horizon is in principle permeable, disruptable, subject to being compromised. The insulation of one horizon from another cannot be assured. The possibility of transformation in the whole orientation one has to a text, or to the other in discussion, is thereby opened up.

These remarks are not incompatible with hermeneutics. It was not by chance that I referred to the *experience* of having one's confident assurances about being understood shattered.[10] There is no hermeneutics without reflection, and if experience itself involves reflection, then no particular experiences can set limits to it.

I have so far tried to show that Derrida's doubts about Gadamer's references to mutual understanding *either* underestimate Gadamer's own stated position (both in 'Text and Interpretation' and in *Truth and Method*) *or* positions one can construct combining Gadamer's own concepts and his more radical tendencies. In this light we can side with Gadamer in his thinking that he is closer to Derrida than Derrida realizes.

Derrida had also asked questions about Gadamer's references to the 'good will'. According to Gadamer 'a written conversation demands basically the same fundamental condition that holds for an oral exchange. Both partners must have the good will to try to understand each other' (corrected translation).[11] Derrida hears echoes of Kant in this reference to the good will. But Derrida's response here fails to do justice either to the problem or to Gadamer's remarks about it. Gadamer's reference to the good will is clearly not to a faculty, nor to the act of a subject, nor to any sort of generalized Nietzschean displacement of disinterestedness. Kant's reference to the good will as the only thing that is good without qualification does indeed seem to be a reference to will. Gadamer's reference can be replaced by expressions that make no reference to a will. We can talk about attitude, orientation or disposition. And here we do not find the reign of the will, but precisely a disposition towards receptivity, an openness to the other. I am most forcibly reminded here not of Kant, but of the Heidegger of *Being and Time* and his references to moods, while Gadamer himself refers to Aristotle. It seems to me that dispositional features are not only free from the obvious traces of logocentrism, but are clearly being deployed to critical ends shared by deconstruction. Derrida knows very well the necessity to recycle metaphysical words, and that modes of articulation, ways of deploying concepts are what counts, not the concepts or terms themselves. Should not Gadamer's demonstration that references to the word 'will' can be dropped be taken seriously? And if we conjoin the two responses I have offered on Gadamer's behalf to Derrida's questions should we not conclude that those questions were somewhat uncharitable? Why, for example, does Derrida treat Levinas so very differently (in 'Violence and Meta-physics'[12])? Levinas is still wedded to a version of phenomenology. If the radical break from the fundamental principle of intentionality that informs this account of the face-to-face relation gains Derrida's respect, why does Derrida not accept that the openness and risk of dialogue that Gadamer insists on is equally a crucial break with Husserl's most logocentric commitments to transcendental solipsism in, for example, his *Cartesian Meditations*? Derrida's long interrogation of Levinas may have seemed critical, but he declared then, and has restated more firmly recently that he has no philosophical disagreement with Levinas. Levinas's project we could call an ethically constitutive displacement of our thinking from the primacy of the subject to the primacy of the other, from wilfulness to openness to the infinity of the other. If Descartes and Kierkegaard had seen the radical dependence of subjectivity on its relation to an absolute other and named it God, Levinas finds that relation first in my relation to you. Derrida himself would not use Levinas's style but does not distance himself from his conclusions. Is it perhaps Gadamer's style or his tone that Derrida responds to?

Derrida's attitude to style is complex. Nietzsche is defended against Heidegger's reading by giving his style a distinctive philosophical weight. Levinas is approved of by discounting his style. Is Gadamer a victim of whim? I think not. Derrida's objection seems fundamentally to be not that Gadamer is committed to a philosophy of presence, though that is what he and Gadamer might agree to call Derrida's view of their disagreement, but that Gadamer is not sufficiently impressed by the power of the radically other, of the otherness of the other. Derrida surely treats Gadamer as someone committed to Hegelian mediation, by which dialogue would serve as an opportunity for each participant either to come to know themselves better by exposure and response, or come to know others better. The return to self would make dialogue an extension of the process of reflection, and would reduce the otherness of the other to being the object of a self-expansive appropriation. Were we to think of dialogue as a means of access to others, we would be committed to treating them, in so far as we could understand them, as alter egos, extensions of ourselves. As I have suggested, Gadamer's reference to the limits of understanding and quite explicitly to the otherness of the other undercuts the motives behind Derrida's response. I claim, then, that in respect of both questions – that of the possibility of understanding the other, and of the good will – a more constructive reading of Gadamer would make Derrida's questions less telling.

Suppose we turn to consider Gadamer's claim about Derrida's performative self-contradiction, that in questioning the drive to mutual understanding and good will, Derrida is himself wanting to be understood. Is there a self-contradiction? Or is there rather (as Gadamer glimpses negatively) a dramatic distantiating enactment of a certain philosophical *vigilance*?

The meaning of an action need not be exhausted by the rules said to constitute that act. (Further significance can be added on.) And even if there is a tight connection between actions and constitutive rules, the precise action one is supposed to be performing is surely open to discussion. Either way, I conclude, Derrida can make the response he did without self-contradiction. What is at issue is not whether Derrida can enter into dialogue with Gadamer but how that action is described or analysed. So I do not think there is a performative contradiction in Derrida responding to Gadamer.

Further, I would like to suggest that Derrida is performing or enacting a certain distantiation or interruption of dialogue in his refusal, as we might say, to *face* Gadamer in full debate.

In his discussions with Labarrière, which focus at one point on the question of ethics, Derrida makes a distinction between two types of relation to the other: *mediation* and *interruption*.[13] Typically, the logic of mediation is one in which the commitment underlying all interaction, all transformation, all development, is to the preservation and restitution of identity. The positions I have described would fit this account.

Derrida identifies this understanding of mediation as Hegelian, and suggests another way of thinking about mediation closer to the formulations of Levinas and Blanchot:

> There is a mediation which does not bar the passage to the other, or to the 'wholly other' [*tout autre*], on the contrary. The rapport to the wholly other as such is a rapport. The relation to the wholly other is a relation.[14]

But things are not that simple. For this relation is like no other, and given that what it relates us to is relationally unavailable, we could call it (Blanchot did) 'a relation [*rapport*] without relation'. Derrida then continues:

> To enter into a relation with the other, interruption must be possible: the relation [*rapport*] must be a relation of interruption. And interruption here does not interrupt the relation to the other, it opens the relation to the other.[15]

He describes this as heralding a different understanding of mediation, which would involve

> a crazy relation [*rapport fou*], a relation [*rapport*] without relation, which understands the other as other in a certain relation of incomprehension. This is not ignorance nor obscurantism nor resignation before any desire for intelligibility: but it is necessary that at a given moment the other remains as other, and that if it is the other it is other: at this moment the relation to the other as such is also the relation of interruption.[16]

The word *interruption* is carefully attuned to its purpose, to capture a break, a rupture, in the *inter*, the *between* by which we relate to the other. It is not an event, in any ordinary sense. One is tempted to say it is a transcendental event. It opens, that is, it makes possible any relation to the other as other. But what is it that is interrupted? If it opens the relation to the other it must always already have happened. I take it he is saying this: that what we think of as a relation to the other is only a relation to the other *as other*, if it builds in some sort of break in our common, appropriative understanding, in which the other is tacitly treated as an alter ego. In the very process of grasping what the other is saying, at the very point of understanding, we must take a step back, allow that movement of assimilation to be interrupted. For Kant, the other should never be treated solely as a means but always as an end in himself or herself. Derrida's way of formulating this would be that it is only when we treat the other as an end that we relate to him *as* an other.

Derrida claims both that interruption must always be possible and that it has always already happened. What this suggests is a complicity between a transcendental condition and an empirical possibility. Grasping the otherness of the other is a condition for my relating to him or her as other, and the reactivation of that grasp must always be possible. And all this must somehow be understood without giving *grasp* any real cognitive status, for that would turn interruption into second order knowledge, rather than marking a limit to knowledge.

This idea of interruption has the forceful implication that certain models of open dialogue are deficient in naively presuming taken-for-granted ways of setting the scene, and ways of anticipating the other. In this light we could see the inadequacy and incompleteness of Derrida's response as a dramatization of the logic of interruption. We know, for example, that Derrida does not accept the implications of openness in the word 'dialogue'. As we shall see, he prefers to talk of *negotiation* as the norm.

We have arrived, at this point, at what we could call an *ethical* moment. To grasp the otherness of the other is not to grasp a *fact* about the other in any ordinary sense, but rather certain universal features of that paradoxical relationship constitutive of what we call 'the other'. The otherness of the other is not a mysterious inaccessible property but a necessary relational truth of a quite different order.

The *transformation* of this insight into a practice is perhaps best thought of as a kind of vigilance. Derrida's response to Gadamer both fails and succeeds in this. By seeming to assimilate Gadamer's position to that of a Hegelian mediation, more appropriate perhaps to Ricoeur,[17] he fails to maintain Gadamer's distinctive difference, he fails to listen properly. By in effect refusing the invitation to what is thought of as an 'open dialogue', he retains an essentially reflexive (and philosophical) vigilance about the underlying assumptions built into such a characterization of philosophical discussion.

Suppose we establish a constructive homology between Derrida and Gadamer on dialogue, there are still difficulties. I would single out the question of teleology. What is the difference between treating total agreement as an aim that is none the less unrealizable, and treating it as a logocentric dream? It is in each case *unrealizable in principle*. But Derrida has a different account – a 'structural' account – of why that is which suggests that philosophical textuality is constitutively structured by a kind of theoretical *incompleteness*, a recognition of an excess which cannot be completely accommodated. For Derrida, Gadamer's dialogue would involve the permanent lure of deepening. For Derrida this 'depth' is an illusion born of the possibility of repetition, by which commentary, response, and so on would repeat the same structures. This *seems* to be a *conclusive* argument. If philosophical texts are characterized by an essential incompleteness and paradoxicality then a certain Olympian distance with regard to the possibilities of dialogue would be understandable.[18] However, it cannot be a conclusive argument until it is recognized as such by others. Put another way, if I am right to think that some such motive underlies Derrida's reserve towards Gadamer, then we surely do have an arguable thesis that is in principle open to denial, acceptance... And saying this does not require that neutral truthfulness will reign.

We are left again with an undecidability: how can we choose between continuing dialogue (with Gadamer) – in which it makes sense to *discuss* Derrida's claims – and reservations (along with Derrida) about the very ideas of dialogue and discussion?

We *might* think it some sort of basic human obligation to submit our views to public scrutiny. But I confess to not seeing any single solution to the difficulties posed by this logical see-saw.

I would like now, briefly, to extend these suggestions to our thinking about the possibilities of human community today. And first, perversely, some conclusions, not mine, but those of Richard Bernstein in two of the papers in his *Philosophical Profiles* (1986).[19] His position could be summed up by saying that while there are important differences between Habermas, Rorty and Gadamer, and even if this is not precisely what they think they are saying to us, each offers us ideals of community and communication which can and should command our best efforts to realize them. These ideals would for example 'allow our social practices to actually become practices where we can engage in rational persuasion and phronesis, rather than manipulation and strategic manoeuvring and where we seek to root out all hidden forms of domination'.[20]

Who could argue against this! It would be like arguing against virtue.

I have already remarked that Derrida has suggested[21] substituting *negotiation* for *dialogue* to emphasize the ineliminability of strategy and force in human communication.[22] This would cut directly into the progressivist ideal. We cannot give a complete argument for Derrida's preferences here – echoes of Nietzsche's references to the will-to-truth, as well as Derrida's own profound suspicion that ideals of 'openness' involve commitments to presence can be clearly heard. But we *could* formulate a minimal version of his point as the claim that we should not protect the values of 'openness','liberation', 'freedom from domination' from the rigour of persistent philosophical scrutiny.

Derrida on this reading is continuing one of the most fundamental traditions of philosophy, that of reflexion. As we argue at length in Chapter 3, 'Deconstruction and Criticism', what is unsettling about his version is that it begins with the very apparatus of philosophy, including all that we take for granted about dialogue, communication, community, etc. It is no accident that in his discussion of Levinas in 'Violence and Metaphysics' he finds in questioning the only possible basis for philosophical community today. I would like to suggest that we are offered now two fundamentally ethical motives for doing something other than practical midwifery to the ideals of open communication and community.

The first is that these ideals are not merely good things that do not yet exist, they are the dreams of philosophers, and the task of reflection on their meaning, value and possibility is never finished. And reflection in and on dialogue is thus inherently problematic. Such reflection is a kind of fundamental philosophical responsibility that one could call ethical. The second motive needs detailed defence and justification: it would translate some of these remarks into the political arena. The drive for consensus presupposes the representability of all views and interests in a common discourse, or some common framework for the exchange of discourses. It involves a reduction of the other to his capacity to represent himself or be represented. This is a presumption required by this socially and politically driven conception of a dialogical community. The success with which particular groups find their voice and join the discussion at the same time legitimates the process that recognizes them. I would not want to slow down this process, indeed I have my own candidates for proper political representation. But it is not without its limitations, limitations which need to be recognized at the very same time as one pursues open and direct communication. For the expansion of community brings with it the danger of assimilation of differences. And here the political and the ethical ideals diverge. For the fundamental ethical difference – the otherness of the other – never gets represented. Indeed it essentially resists representation. I do not want to deny the enormous strides made by liberal or critical or progressive humanism. But it is not the philosopher's job either to cheer on the course of history, or to change the track settings, but to remind us of what we may have forgotten in our virtuous enthusiasm for openness.

Notes

1   A colloquium on *Text and Interpretation* was held at the Goethe Institute in Paris in April 1981, 'bringing together' Gadamer and Derrida.

2   Diane Michelfelder and Richard Palmer (eds), *Dialogue and Deconstruction* (hereafter *DD*) (Albany: SUNY, 1989) is the best example.

3   What is perhaps not evident from his treatment in this paper is that he has a rather distinct treatment of literary texts – as radically cut off from their authors, speaking on their own behalf, allowing language to speak as language, which only appeared later in an extended printed version of the paper.

4   *DD*, p. 57.

5   ibid., p. 57.

6   Gadamer introduces the idea of the fusion of horizons in *Truth and Method* (London: Sheed & Ward, 1960). Understanding an object requires the fusion of the object's horizon with that of the interpreter.

7   Text and Interpretation, in *DD*, p. 26.

8   ibid., p. 25.

9   For Gadamer, application is an essential moment of interpretation, in which meaning is actually filled out and determined, and not just 'applied' in some technical sense. See, for example, Gadamer's discussion of the interpretation of law in *Truth and Method*, pp. 294ff.

10   The closest Gadamer gets to this shattering is in his discussion of works of art in *Truth and Method*.

11   *DD*, p. 33.

12 In *Writing and Difference* [1967] (Chicago: Chicago University Press 1978), pp. 79–153.
13 Jacques Derrida and Pierre-Jean Labarrière, *Alterités* (Paris: Osiris, 1986).
14 ibid., p. 82.
15 ibid.
16 ibid.
17 I am thinking of Ricoeur's understanding of reading and discussion as the necessary detour, the long road to self-understanding. See for example his essay 'Appropriation', in *Hermeneutics and the Human Sciences*, trans John Thompson (Cambridge: Cambridge University Press, 1981).
18 I associate such a position with that constructed for Derrida by Gasché in his *The Tain of the Mirror* (Cambridge, Mass.: Harvard University Press, 1986).
19 'What is the difference that makes a difference? Gadamer, Rorty and Habermas', and 'From hermeneutics to praxis', in R. Bernstein (ed.) *Philosophical Profiles* (Cambridge: Polity Press, 1986). These papers date from 1982.
20 *Philosophical Profiles*, p. 93.
21 In Derrida and Labarrière, *Alterités*.
22 It would be well worth comparing Sartre's critique of the idea of sincerity in *Being and Nothingness* [1943] (London: Methuen, 1957).

Further reading

The central methodological dispute here is between hermeneutics and deconstruction. We have already suggested (see 'Further reading' for Chapter 3) reading on deconstruction. There is a useful source-book on hermeneutics edited by Kurt Mueller-Vollmer, *The Hermeneutics Reader* (Oxford: Blackwell, 1986). Paul Ricoeur's *Hermeneutics and the Human Sciences*, ed. John Thompson (Cambridge: Polity Press, 1981) collects some fine essays. There are two excellent collections of critical essays: R. Hollinger (ed.), *Hermeneutics and Praxis* (Notre Dame: Notre Dame University Press, 1985) and Hugh J. Silverman and Don Ihde (eds), *Hermeneutics and Deconstruction* (Albany: SUNY, 1985). Apart from Gadamer's *magnum opus Truth and Method* (London: Sheed & Ward, [1960] 1975) his *Philosophical Hermeneutics* (Berkeley and Los Angeles: University of California Press, 1976) contains some excellent essays on the scope of hermeneutical reflection and on Heidegger and phenomenology. On the subject of dialogue, his eight hermeneutical studies of Plato, *Dialogue and Dialectic* (New Haven: Yale University Press, 1980), are worth reading.

On the particular debate between Derrida and Gadamer, the essential reading is *The Gadamer–Derrida Encounter: Texts and Commentary* (see note 2).

8

Performative reflexivity

In London in 1986 Jacques Derrida gave a two-hour lecture entitled 'Philosophy before the Law'.[1] Afterwards I heard two respected members of the philosophical community agreeing between them that it was 'garbage', a judgement later communicated to me directly. Now, the most thoughtful response to this judgement would be not to reject it outright but rather to ponder its possible senses and associations. Garbage is what is thrown out, rejected. And Derrida is, indeed, very often picking up on interpretations, possibilities, associations that philosophy has thrown out, or rejected, or refused. Perhaps the connection between garbage and refuse should be further explored.[2]

However, my actual reply to this dismissive judgement was to begin by saying that it was not an intellectually respectable response. So they expanded on it. He was self-indulgent. He had given too many interpretations of Kafka's short story. And some of these interpretations had gone on too long, long after he had 'made the point'. And was the psychoanalytical reading and were the pointed references to Freud really necessary? Finally, how had he dared to talk for two hours?

It remains my suspicion that his real crime was to speak for two hours. But the thrust or drift of my reply was that these critics had misunderstood not so much what he was saying, but what he was doing. They missed the structure of reflexivity in the very form of the lecture, which offers a number of different readings of Kafka's story, while withholding the interpretive verdict. For this withholding directly reflects one of the key features of the story under discussion ('Before the Law') in which an innocent man (from the country) is refused entry to 'the Law'. Derrida is withholding from his audience the key to the text in just the same way, and yet by virtue of this reflexive parallel he is actually suggesting an interpretation for 'the Law', namely, the demand that a text have a meaning. They also missed the fact that Derrida is not concerned just to arrive at certain results, but publicly to enact the process of getting there, what Heidegger would call 'letting truth show itself', letting us participate in the writing.

Nietzsche would say my friends lacked ears. My claim is that if they had grasped these performative qualities of the lecture, they might still have been hungry at the end of the two hours, but not quite as angry.

In this chapter I want to approach the question of philosophy as performance. Not theatrical ways of presenting lectures but the ways in which philosophical writing in general exhibits performative qualities, which one ignores at one's peril.

But first some brief analytical or definitional notes.

First, of the many possible definitions of performance I prefer this: a performative mode of writing is one in which what takes place is dependent on a reflexive strategy, in which the object of reflection is the nature and limits of writing itself, or of a particular practice of writing (such as philosophy).

Second, the term 'performance' has here at least three confluent associations: (1) the idea of a complex staging – philosophy being treated as a meld of action and event (for example, when one says that a certain book intervenes in a debate); (2) the connection with dance – or the sort of dance in which there is some fusion (or perhaps con-fusion) of style and content, form and meaning; and (3) Austin's analytical account of performative speech-acts as acts in which something is done rather than merely said (such as 'I undertake to finish this book by April', which, under the right conditions etc., constitutes a promise).

It is no doubt possible to give some account of the performative aspect of any philosophical work. A traditional form would concern itself with its rhetorical stratum, the devices designed to persuade or to lull, to win over the reader. Even a glittering display of logical formalism might be treated in this way. The value of such a study would be largely defensive. One would learn how to detect the ploys of the seducer, the soft lights and music of philosophical demonstration, and so learn the point at which to resist, to be sceptical.

But there are some works in which the performative aspect transcends the level of rhetorical adornment, in which the way the work is written is one of the central focuses of the philosophical task in which it is engaged, if not *the* central focus. Doubtless it is possible, once the suggestion has been made, to come to see that this is true for a growing number of philosophical works. And such an expansion of vision is to be welcomed. But I would like here to concentrate on the work of four philosophers – Kierkegaard, Nietzsche, Heidegger and Derrida – in whose work the performative dimension most marked their own practice of 'writing'.

People have wide-ranging reactions to this list. Some still insist that they are not real philosophers at all, some that they are enormously difficult, while for others they are the most fascinating, rich and provocative thinkers of the last two centuries. I will try to explain why they are difficult, why the question of whether they are philosophers is not a simple either/or, and how the way they write is the consequence of a train of thoughts which can be expressed in the form of an argument. Indeed, there is a sense in which each 'philosopher' viewed his choice of a way of writing as necessary. To explain this necessity I have to show how each of them held a thesis about the limits of philosophical discourse. I argue that a concern with the question of the limits of philosophy is not a sign of hysteria but an essential mark of intellectual integrity, quite as much today as ever it was.

I am not an apologist for all obscure and difficult writing, nor even for everything these particular philosophers have written. What I would like to show is that there is a vital dimension of their writing, which I call *performative reflexivity*, which if ignored or misunderstood will impede an adequate response to it. So much of my task will be devoted to reconstructing the form of this reflexivity, offering arguments for accepting the premises involved, and some judgements about the value of this philosophical writing.

To illustrate and begin to explore this reflexivity I will focus attention on short passages from Heidegger and Derrida respectively. We will find here, writ large, structures more usually developed on a wider canvas.

In his essay 'Language' ('Die Sprache' 1950) Heidegger discusses for the most part a poem by Georg Trakl: 'A Winter Evening'. He begins by suggesting that the essence of language might better be found in poetry rather than in ordinary writing or speech. A poem is what he calls a pure form of speaking. And it is to follow through this idea that he turns to Trakl. Let us look at the first four lines of the poem (in Hofstadter's translation)

> Window with falling snow is arrayed
> Long tolls the vesper bell.

The house is provided well,
The table is for many laid.[3]

Before Heidegger quotes these lines he has offered as a guiding assertion that 'Language speaks' which he will be using the poem to try to justify and explain. Heidegger's question (immediately preceding the poem) is 'What is it to speak?' And from the context we know that Heidegger is asking for an answer with something like an onto-logical ring to it. His first attempt to answer it (*PLT*, p. 198) goes like this

The speaking names the winter evening time. What is this naming? Does it merely deck out the imaginable familiar events – snow, bell, window, falling, ringing – with words of a language? No, this naming does not hand out titles, it does not apply terms, but it calls into the word. The naming calls. Calling brings closer what it calls . . .

Heidegger is not only interpreting Trakl's poem so as to bring out the way his words illuminate the world they refer to, but the peculiar way in which Heidegger describes the word/world relation – 'calling into the word' – also describes what he is himself *practising* at the interpretive level. That is, the move from naming to calling, and on a later page to bidding and inviting, is in each case itself a move that calls us, bids us, invites us to see naming and referring in a certain way – not simply as applying words to things pre-cut , but as giving things a linguistic embodiment. The use of the terms 'naming', 'calling', 'bidding', 'inviting' is unusual, creative and suggestive and structurally replicates the use of language in Trakl's poem, which he is bringing out by the use of these terms.

Where is Heidegger going? 'We do not want to get anywhere. We would like only, for once, to get to just where we are already' (*PLT*, p. 190) Elsewhere he talks of bringing us 'face to face with a possibility of undergoing an experience with language'.[4] We already speak language. That is where we are at already. But, he claims, we have to undergo an experience with language to understand what that accomplishment really involves, namely, a *dwelling* prior to any accomplishment.

Heidegger here uses language in a way that he takes to exemplify our true relation to language, and to do so in the course of showing how a poet uses language in just such an authentic way.

Another example of this reflective performance, in which the writing itself provides internal evidence of the possibility that it itself describes, can be found in Heidegger's (1935/6) essay 'The Origin of the Work of Art'.[5] In this essay Heidegger describes the work-being of a work (what makes a work of art a work) as its ability to 'open up a world' to us; the work of art 'allows truth to happen'. In each case he is talking about *great* works of art. If this essay seems difficult it is because he is introducing us to a way of thinking about how art works, a way that can itself best be described as 'opening a world', 'allowing truth to happen' and so on. He is engaged in producing a work that exemplifies the features it itself attributes to works of art *qua* works.

Analogous structures of reflexive performance can be found in Derrida's writing. Take for instance the first pages of his essay 'The *retrait* of metaphor'.[6] I will quote fragments from the first two pages.

> What is happening (Qu'est-ce qui se passe . . .), today, with metaphor? . . . It is a very old subject. It occupies the West, inhabits or lets itself be inhabited: representing itself there as an enormous library in which we could move about without perceiving its limits, proceeding from station to station, going on foot, step by step . . . Metaphor circulates – in the city, it conveys us like its inhabitants, along all sorts of passages . . . We are in a certain way – metaphorically of course, and as concerns the mode of habitation – the content and tenor of this vehicle: passengers, comprehended and displaced by metaphor . . .

As we saw in Chapter 2 ('Metaphysics and Metaphor') in this and his other writings on metaphor (such as 'White Mythology') Derrida is attempting both to demonstrate the pervasiveness of metaphor in philosophy, and also to undermine any suggestion that we could simply reduce philosophy to the status of a metaphorical discourse. One reason we cannot perform such a reduction – a reason crucial to 'The *retrait* of metaphor' – is that the whole idea of metaphor is historically linked with the idea of a proper meaning, or the proper application of a word, in relation to which a metaphor would be a displacement. Derrida claims that such a notion (the proper meaning) is a metaphysical notion. For the very concept of metaphor is strictly speaking bound up with a certain philosophical commitment to a privileged proper object for a name, and so could not itself perform a foundational role for philosophy, being already implicated in philosophical distinctions and considerations.

So much by way of background. What is happening here? First of all there are a few hidden allusions. The first line: 'What is happening, today, with metaphor?' is surely a transformation of a line of Heidegger's 'How does it stand with Being?'[7] To begin with such a substitutive transformation is to do a number of things at once. It is to suggest a link to Heidegger in the course of a move away from him. It suggests in particular a displacement of Heidegger's concern with deepening our understanding of being, in favour of the mobility of metaphor. And it suggests, as we immediately see confirmed, an interest in the whole idea of displacement. In the first full paragraph Derrida gets carried away into a discourse on transportation. We find here a play between words of place (occupies, inhabits, inhabitants) and words of movement (move about, proceeding, circulates, translation, transportation, and so on). And it is not just language that is caught up in this play, but us. We are passengers, comprehended and displaced by metaphor. The references to 'the West' and to the enormous (Borgesian?) library are intended to remind us of a thesis that can be credited to both Nietzsche and Heidegger that the history of philosophy can be circumscribed as a finite field of possible positions and moves 'in which we would move about without perceiving its limits'.

By this play on words of place and words of movement, Derrida brings to the surface the opposition traditionally constitutive of the concept of metaphor. With the suggestion that we are caught up in such play he not only throws into doubt our sense of control over language, but also our sense of self-understanding. And he also makes use of the notion of displacement – a notion central to metaphor – to capture our new position in relation to metaphor. Subjectivity is displaced by the all-pervasiveness of metaphorical displacement. And finally, the importance of this notion of all-pervasiveness comes in understanding the kind of lucidity (or lack of it) that we have in relation to the limits of our own (philosophical) enterprise.

A little later in the same essay he makes some of these moves explicit. In addition he reflects on the metaphorical status of this discussion of metaphor and concludes that we cannot just say that such terms as 'transportation' are metaphors (nor merely literal). More interestingly for us, he begins to reflect on his own power to avoid being taken over by the subject with which he is dealing. This is a simple reflexive application of the point made above that as Nietzsche put it: 'the most diverse philosophers always fill in again a definite fundamental scheme of possible philosophies. Under an invisible spell, they always revolve once more in the same orbit.'[8]

If the notion of metaphor displaces the idea of the subject – the controlling, directing author, who should rather be seen as subjected to the workings of the metaphorical field within which he/she is writing – then do these considerations not apply to *this* discourse? About metaphor, Derrida writes:

> I cannot *treat it* without *dealing with it*, without negotiating with it the loan that I take from it in order to speak of it. I did not succeed in producing a *treatise* on metaphor which is not *treated with* metaphor . . . That is why just now I have been moving from digression to digression from one vehicle to another without being able to brake or to stop the autobus, its automaticity, or its automobility . . .

And, he adds

> The drama, for this is a drama, is that even if I had decided to no longer speak metaphorically about metaphor, I would not achieve it. It would continue to go on without me in order to make me speak, to ventriloquize me, metaphorise me.[9]

What Derrida is saying in these reflexive remarks is that the loss of control evident in the first two pages is only a graphic expression of the impossibility of complete authorial control, and especially when one is 'dealing with' such a fundamental question as metaphor. As he suggests, we have to 'do a deal with metaphor', rather than strive for some vain mastery from a neutral non-metaphorical stand-point. And even when he reflects on this lack of control, it appears again in the skidding text with which he explains it. I want, for a moment, to apply the brakes to this discussion of Derrida. It was designed only to offer a taste of the kind of difficulty in reading a text to which I first referred. The difficulty arises firstly from the allusiveness of the text (the parodic though serious allusion to Heidegger might not be obvious to all), the extreme 'self-consciousness' of the writing, which appears especially in the form of self-commentary, and lastly the pervasive performative reflexivity of the writing, in which Derrida is constantly exhibiting at work in his own writing the very limits and moves and structures about which he is writing. There are obvious problems with this last procedure. To put it most sharply, in order for one's textual performance to have philosophical value, it must convince the reader that it demonstrates a general truth, rather than an idiosyncratic one about the difficulties Derrida experiences in reining in his wild pen. What we have to be convinced of is that the artifice of the Derridean theatre holds a lesson for all writing.[10]

I would like now to show how the stage was set for this performative textuality by two predecessors of Heidegger and Derrida, namely Kierkegaard and Nietzsche. (Kierkegaard's direct influence may be confined here to Heidegger.)

It is hard to read a serious slice of Kierkegaard's work without being impressed by the prolific variety of his stylistic repertoire. He wrote dialectically, sometimes (but not always) in deliberate parody of Hegel. He made use of the narrative form, he wrote edifying discourses, he preached, he mocked, he wrote diatribes against the established church, he wrote works of 'psychology'. But as well as exploiting this diversity of genres, he often masked his authorship with a range of pseudonyms, to which are attached authorial poses.

In Chapter 6, I discussed Kierkegaard's claim that the only true communication is indirect. For Hegel, we may recall, 'Truth is only realized in the form of a system', and once a part of that system becomes detached from it (for example, a particular proposition) it ceases to have a truth value. Hegel's vivid image is that of a Bacchanalian revel in which the drunken dancers all hold each other up. As soon as you are detached from the circle you collapse. This may help to dispel any idea of the system as a static whole, but even in this dynamic form, Kierkegaard would have none of it. Truth begins and ends in subjectivity. Kierkegaard argues from this position to the conclusion (one that explains and justifies much of the way he writes) that the only true communication is indirect.

The argument is something like this: We can and must make a distinction between objective and subjective thought. Objective thought is concerned only with results (the discovery of truths) while subjective thinking is thinking as a process in which an existing individual is concernfully engaged. Now both forms of thinking involve reflection – objective thought abstracts reflectively from a particular situation in order to apply concepts, but subjectivity involves a double reflection. The second stage, which distinguishes subjective thinking, is what he calls 'its reflection of inwardness, or of possession, by virtue of which it belongs to the thinking subject and to no one else'. Kierkegaard's crucial claim is that direct communication (just saying what one believes) is incapable of capturing this double reflection. Direct communication is constitutionally unfit to express the subject's engagement with his own thought, the fact that his thought is a process, a thinking, and never done with, and that it is all these things precisely to the extent that it is not given outward expression. (He gives the example of feelings of love which are too tender and too incomplete to be able to survive public expression.) Kierkegaard does not deny the possibility of communication of subjectivity, but he puts a limitation on it. It can only be done indirectly: 'This form should embody artistically as much of reflection as he himself has when existing in his thought. In an artistic manner please note; for the secret does not lie in a direct assertion of the double reflection.'[11]

Obviously the classic mode of indirectness is that of irony, to which Kierkegaard devotes a whole book. But equally, one could point to his use of pseudonyms, by which he allows himself, if only for pedagogical purposes to take up as an author positions that he himself had transcended.[12] I argued that we have to understand indirect communication not just as a relation between subjectivity and linguistic expression. The point of indirect communication is not merely that the communicating subject transmit to the other the fact of his or her subjectivity, but, just as important, the reader has to go though the same moves that the writer went through. And in going through these moves one acquaints oneself with one's own inwardness, and is thereby emancipated from self-objectification.

Derrida's writing, for all the divergence in his philosophical agenda, none the less involves a reflexivity which is formally very similar.[13] The obvious point of difference is that for Derrida the value Kierkegaard gives to subjectivity betrays a metaphysical privileging of inwardness, the privilege of self-presence. And yet there is no doubt that Derrida's practice is designed to bring the reader to re-enact the same sorts of moves that Derrida himself makes as a writer, and thus come to realize the naivety of certain philosophical positions (for example, the reduction of philosophy to metaphor, however liberating such a move may initially seem).

One can even come to wonder whether the play without end that is writing, writing seen as incapable of stemming its own flow, or bringing about textual closure, might not be thought rather a transposition of everything Kierkegaard says about subjectivity. Might not the reasons for Kierkegaard's difficulty in expressing subjectivity directly be analogous to the problems of summarizing the meaning of a piece of writing, of capturing, pinning down its sense, pretending one could cut short its possibilities of play? If writing, as Derrida understands it, includes the entire universe of articulated signs, would not Kierkegaard's subjectivity be included as a kind of writing – perhaps not privileged in the way Kierkegaard suggests, but at least incapable of a complete translation into some other medium. If I might be permitted the liberty of rewriting, it would be quite appropriate to say of Derrida that his writing fulfils the maxim that 'This form should embody artistically as much of reflection as he himself has when *writing*. In an artistic manner please note; for the secret does not lie in a direct assertion of the *reflexive strategy*' (adapted from *Concluding Unscientific Postscript*, pp. 68–9).

Nietzsche too wrote in a myriad of styles.[14] It is not because none satisfied him that he kept changing his style. For Nietzsche, the inadequacy of any one style was a matter of principle. Straightforward, declarative, descriptive language only nourished the old philosophical illusion of the representational adequacy of language. But it is not the natural function of language to represent the world, nor is it capable of doing so. Representation is just a philosopher's dream (perhaps the dream of philosophy). The point of multiplying one's styles is to draw attention to style. And the point of drawing attention to style is to focus on the way language is used, for with the illusion of representation out of the way, what matters is how language is used.

Kierkegaard had said: 'The objective accent falls on *What* is said; the subjective accent on *How* it is said' (*CUP*, p. 81). And without perhaps endorsing the term 'subjective', Nietzsche would have agreed. Nietzsche's description of his own style as 'an overleaping mockery of symmetries' is most apparent in his aphoristic passages. He recommends that philosophers should dance with their pens, that they should forsake the spirit of seriousness, and recognize language for what it is, an expression of the will to power, and governed by aesthetic rather than epistemological values. Nietzsche too, it is clear, has an emancipatory intent, even though he suggests that he is writing for an audience that does not exist. The implication is not just that his contemporaries could not understand him, but that they were not prepared to participate in the text in the way Nietzsche required. We could give the name participation to the uptake that

Kierkegaard was trying to bring about. For Nietzsche, while there was a real sense in which he solicits a participatory response – one has very often to complete the thought begun by an aphorism – he also aims to have an effect, that of unsettling his reader's assured familiarity with traditional philosophical concepts. At one point he tells us to distrust all inherited concepts. His overleaping mockery of conceptual symmetries is designed to encourage such distrust, in much the same way as Derrida's play with metaphors of transport, slipping and braking, is intended to undermine our assurance that we, as subjects, can keep ourselves aloof from this play.

If we are right this common concern with performative reflexivity knits Kierkegaard and Nietzsche together with Heidegger and Derrida into a tradition. The recognition that there is a tradition of writing in this way ought at least to give us pause before we dismiss them as too difficult (or worse).

But we can still return with the question: even if I can now understand roughly *what* they are doing, *why* do they do it? And how necessary is it all? Is it not rather a kind of affectation that a bit of immersion in no-nonsense British philosophy would long ago have cured them?

I want now to offer a general argument which, if successful, will lead us to think of the transformation of philosophical style into a performance as an attractive if not compelling option. We shall then be in a better position to assess the artificiality or otherwise of these strategies. I shall argue that these strategies are of real philosophical value, although they offer no guarantees of success, and that the premises on which they are based are not to be dismissed lightly. This general argument probably applies more to Derrida (and Nietzsche) than to Heidegger. The basic premise is one we can find in a number of places in Nietzsche and in Derrida. In Chapter 5, 'Nietzsche's Styles', I called it the thesis of the closure of philosophy. I distinguished two main forms in Nietzsche, which I call the structural and the dialectical forms. In the structural version Nietzsche observes 'how unfailingly the most diverse Philosophers always fill in again a definite fundamental scheme of possible philosophies' within an orbit prescribed by 'the unconscious domination and guidance of similar grammatical functions'.[15] Philosophy is essentially repetition, and its sharpest analytical tools rest on linguistic and physiological conditions open neither to inspection nor reflection.

On the second, dialectical model, to be found in his account of 'How the Real World Became a Myth',[16] Nietzsche reduces the history of philosophy to six stages (and two pages). As we have seen, what mutates at each stage is the status of what is thought of as the *real world*, beginning with Plato's position, in which it was only accessible to the philosopher, and ending with the recognition that with the disappearance of the real world, what is contrasted with it, the world of appearances also disappears. Here begins the age of Zarathustra, and the end of illusion.

The importance of this thesis, in either of its two forms, is that to the thinker who accepts it, it immediately poses the problem of how to respond. My claim will be that performative reflexivity is a rational solution. The important thing here is that this thesis – the closure of philosophy thesis – is a thesis held in one form or another by Heidegger and Derrida. (And arguably it was the suggestion that Hegel had brought thought to its completion that inspired Kierkegaard.) I described Heidegger and Derrida as each holding the thesis 'in one form or other'. Heidegger's position is first found in *Being and Time* (1927). Here he lays out the ontological dimensions of human existence, announcing the ground-clearing task of destroying the history of ontology (Section 6). The aim of this procedure is not in fact destructive, but rather one of making 'the history of Being transparent'. This is to be brought about by loosening up its hardened tradition, and dissolving the concealments it has brought about. What we arrive at are 'those primordial experiences in which we achieved our first ways of determining the nature of Being', that is, a process of historical anamnesis.

Heidegger later came to see that he could not allow himself to treat human existence as a privileged source of primordial experiences somehow unsoiled by history. For wherever he turned language followed. And language seemed to be implicated from the start in the metaphysical history that he had diagnosed. For metaphysical concepts, oppositions, grammatical forms are found in ordinary language, not merely abstract philosophical theory. And yet if that is so, if, as Nietzsche suggested, the closure of philosophy is a consequence of secret deep-structural features of our language, what possible form can resistance to that influence take? Heidegger's move, of which we have already seen a sample, was often to take up the thoughts of German philosophical poets, poets who themselves reflected poetically on language and its limits. He addresses them in a sensitive and responsive way, in which there are clear echoes of philosophical theories but which carefully resists the traditional ways of giving voice to them. Heidegger, as we have said, seeks to awaken a new experience with language; not a new view of language, but a new relation to it. And he does so by an exemplary performance. He writes in such a way as to demonstrate such a new relation. One very specific relational change he aims at, one which Derrida (in 'The *retrait* of metaphor') clearly endorses, and one which most effectively demonstrates the value of a performative 'solution', is to bring an end to the domination of a writing and speaking in which language is treated as an instrument, as a means, a transparent vehicle of a thought that could in principle be formulated in some independent medium. If Heidegger seems sometimes too precious, too self-conscious, it is because he tries to practise not merely, with Nietzsche, a 'suspicion' of inherited concepts, but rather a reverential savouring and exploration of them. He fastens on to the words he finds himself to have used, he draws out their etymological possibilities, he avoids simplifications of thought that would slip him back into metaphysical ruts.

Without some sort of grasp of the closure of philosophy thesis, this enterprise must seem almost unintelligible. And, moreover, unless one has some understanding of what Heidegger means by the overcoming of metaphysics, the status of his writing will be almost impossible to assess. For Heidegger, overcoming metaphysics does not mean putting it aside, moving on to something else, but something more like an incorporation that opens up a new beginning. And this beginning is best understood as a new form of (meditative) thinking.

Derrida, on the other hand, inherits the thesis of the closure of metaphysics from Nietzsche, through Heidegger, but at the same time he sees the enormous methodological problems that such a thesis poses for any discipline that might in some sense succeed philosophy, or, in different terms, that it poses for a non-metaphysical philosophy.

Derrida's version of the closure thesis is that the history of philosophy is the history of the philosophy of presence, the belief in privileged points of reference. For Derrida, what is true of any 'sign' – that it is constituted by its differential relations to other signs – is true of any supposed value of presence (he mentions idea, the now, intuition, intersubjectivity ...) and thus undermines its alleged purity and originality. If philosophy as we know it is constituted by appeal to such values, it would suggest either the need for a step outside philosophy, or the development of a new critical method dedicated to unearthing these appeals to 'presence'. But such a critique is not without its difficulties. For if you suppose, as Derrida does, that the most powerful tools for criticism are ones which belong to the very history one is trying to undermine, then a programme of deconstruction might seem only to be what is called an immanent critique. However such internal criticism threatens to change nothing at all. If one affirms certain critical terms by the very fact of using them, then one merely establishes a new orthodoxy. Derrida diagnoses the situation as one in which we have to transform a field of discourse, while the means available constantly tend to reconfirm it.

Perhaps, as the saying goes, it is a change of style that we need, or a change of strategy.

In Kierkegaard's case, it was the double reflexivity characteristic of subjectivity that set the requirement for indirect communication. The crucial feature of the second level of reflection is engagement, involvement, commitment in one's own thinking, and thinking as an ongoing process, not capturable as a set of 'results'. Kierkegaard's problem could be regarded as an ethical one. Derrida's problem is one of boundary strategy and methodology. It is the problem of how to 'bear in mind', to take seriously, the closure of philosophy thesis without quite abandoning philosophy. His solution is to opt for an obsessive anti-naivety or 'self-consciousness' or 'reflexivity' in writing. This is sustained by something approximating a theory of language, and an explicit rejection of any model in which language would have the status of an instrument or a means for the transmission of independently formulable thoughts. For Kierkegaard, indirect communication is a reflexive performance that points back to a silence – the subjectivity of the writer – and releases an awareness of subjectivity on the part of the reader. For Derrida on the other hand reflexivity does not point to a simple outside or beyond the text, but to the medium and practice of writing itself; to Kierkegaardian commitment or engagement corresponds the essential embodiment of one's articulated thought – in writing. And it is that fact to which, by extension, a performative reflexivity would point.

As Derrida sees it, the situation of the philosopher is this: that the traditional 'values' of philosophy, the values to which it appeals (truth, objectivity, reality, intuition, and so on) are none of them simple unities, independent of language but always appear worked up into a syntax – in the simplest form, that of a weighted opposition (e.g. truth/fiction, literal/metaphorical, objectivity/subjectivity). If this is right, there is no philosophical value not already implicated in that articulation we call writing. So when the philosopher appeals to truth, or even to subjectivity, as Kierkegaard does, he or she is not appealing to something beyond writing, but making a move within writing.

Now whether or not we accept this claim or even understand precisely what accepting it would involve, one can see that it puts considerable pressure on precisely how one writes philosophy. No more can one pretend that one's words don't fully capture one's meaning. Rather such a claim would itself be treated as a desire, the desire for presence, the vain desire that the endless wording should come to an end.

If performative reflexivity reaches its peak in Derrida, it becomes clearer why one might claim that a performative mode of writing is one in which what takes place is dependent on a reflective strategy the 'object of which is the nature and limits of writing itself'.

I have claimed that performative reflexivity is a rationally motivated strategy. I shall now try to reconstruct this motivation in the form of an argument:

1 Philosophy as a whole or in large part can be circumscribed in a way which imposes unsuspected and unacceptable limits on its scope or power (the closure of philosophy thesis).
2 This delimitation undermines a certain sort of dream, or desire, expressed perhaps in common references to 'capturing reality'.
3 Such a dream is embodied in the view of language as an inherently representational medium.
4 Language cannot be plausibly held to be the natural servant of epistemology.
5 The ideal of a (philosophical) text that would demystify or enlighten us *in the name of truth* is no longer credible.
6 What is still possible – and indeed necessary if something like philosophy is to continue – is a mode of writing which, while grafted on to traditional epistemological stock, productively questions those fundamental assumptions.

The fact that there is something of a tradition of people making this performative move doesn't make the move necessary. And surely there are alternative responses to the discovery of the intimate connection between philosophy and language?

If one thought the defects of philosophy were rooted in ordinary everyday language one might think that something like Carnap's programme of formalization was the answer. But in order to know whether one had solved a certain philosophical problem by formalization, one would have to have a rule to decide whether the translation into the formal language was one in which the problem had been sufficiently retained to be solved. It is hard to see what such a rule would look like, or where it would belong, and arguably if the problem can be solved in the formal but not in the everyday language then we must be dealing with a different problem.

It might be thought that analytic philosophy is essentially neutral with regard to the old metaphysical issues, but it is not neutral with regard to language. It believes in the possibility of separating a term's meaning (or proper use) from the various associations the term might have. And that seems to rest on refusing to question the traditional distinction between essential and accidental properties.

One might want instead to plunge after the later Wittgenstein into the detailed contextuality of our use of language, eschewing analytical generalizations, but this would mean leaving the classical philosophical texts out in the sun to perish. Derrida's philosophical strategy allows him to practise an interventionist reading of classical texts, rather than just leaving them behind. No such list of objections to the alternatives could ever show the necessity of the Derridean alternative. But I suspect that many who see what Derrida is doing and do not follow him do not so much reject the logic of the argument (such as it is) but rather the premisses on which it rests. 'What value does this performative reflexivity have?' 'What is the point of it?' These are very difficult issues. One might begin by questioning the classical form ('What is ...?') or the terms. It is not sophistry to say that an adequate response would address the classical form of the question 'What is...?',[17] and would ask about *value* and *point*. Such interruption is always essentially possible, and the *value* of such interruptions lies perhaps in the challenge they pose to our traditional modes of philosophizing, and in the consistency and resolution with which Derrida practises this strategy. One thing we can learn both from Derrida and from Heidegger is an enormous reflective sensitivity to the philosophical language we all use.

There is, however, a general doubt or objection to the whole language of performance and reflexivity. In *Allegories of Reading*,[18] Paul de Man draws out of Nietzsche's writing the need to move from a constative or declarative model of language to a performative one, with direct implications for philosophical strategy. But at the same time he shows Nietzsche to be deconstructing any account of *performance* that would simply reproduce the metaphysical categories of subject and act. This is quite right. If the language of performance is to further our thinking it must, precisely, become the site of the dehiscence and interrogation of these categories. Performance is not an act under a subject's intentional control. It is a perhaps temporary locus for the deconstructive reworking of these very terms. Nor is *reflexivity* to be thought of as a route to a more complex self-appropriation. It is precisely the operation that, as it deepens, opens up *abysses*. Perhaps deconstruction announces the limit of philosophy in its necessary but productive interminability.

Notes

1 February 1986, at the Royal Institute of Philosophy.
2 Jonathan Culler's review of Michael Thompson's *Rubbish Theory (Diacritics*, vol. 15, no. 3, fall 1985, pp. 2–14) would be a good place to start.
3 *Poetry, Language, Thought* [hereafter *PLT*], trans. A. Hofstadter, (New York: Harper & Row, 1971), p. 194.
4 'The Nature of Language', in *On the Way to Language* [1959], trans. P. D. Hertz (New York: Harper & Row, 1971), p. 57.
5 This can be found in *PLT*.
6 Trans. in *Enclitic*, vol. 11, no. 2, (fall 1978).
7 Heidegger, *An Introduction to Metaphysics*, (London: Doubleday, [1953] 1961), pp. 26 ff.
8 *Beyond Good and Evil* (New York: Vintage [1885] 1966), Section 26.
9 'The *retrait* of metaphor', *Enclitic*, vol. II, no. 2 (fall 1978), pp. 7–8.
10 See Irene Harvey, *Derrida and the Economy of Différance* (Bloomington: Indiana University Press, 1986), pp. 55 f.
11 *Concluding Unscientific Postscript* [hereafter *CUP*], trans. D. F. Swanson (Princeton University Press, 1968), pp. 68–9.
12 His confession and key to these pseudonyms is to be found at the end of the work cited – *Concluding Unscientific Postscript*.
13 A more systematic study of this comparison has been made by S. Agacinski, *Aparté* (Tallahassee: Florida State University Press, 1988).
14 I am drawing here on the analysis in Chapter 5, 'Nietzsche's Styles'.
15 *Beyond Good and Evil*, Section 20.
16 *Twilight of the Idols*, trans. R. J. Hollingdale (Harmondsworth: Penguin, 1968).
17 See Derrida's *Of Spirit* [1987], trans. G. Bennington and R. Bowlby (Chicago: Chicago University Press, 1989), e.g. pp. 14 f.
18 Paul de Man, *Allegories of Reading* (New Haven: Yale University Press, 1979), Chapter 6, 'Rhetoric of Persuasion (Nietzsche)', pp. 124 f.

Further reading

The specifically Derridean contribution to the relation between textual performance and the limits of language is best pursued further through his reading of Blanchot, particularly the latter's *Le Pas au-delà* (The Step [Not] Beyond) (Paris: Gallimard, 1973). See especially Derrida's 'Pas' [1976], in *Parages* (Paris: Galilée 1986). An excellent introduction to these questions can be found in Herman Rapaport's *Heidegger and Derrida: Reflections on Time and Language* (Lincoln: University of Nebraska, 1989).

Conclusion:
the theatre of difficulty

This book is a contribution to the radical problematization of the bounda-ries, thresholds and brinks to which philosophical inquiry is inevitably driven. Such liminology is informed by two distinct suppositions. The first is that the image of breakthrough to a philosophical 'beyond' is a mirage, a shimmering invitation to walk into a mirror in which are reflected the artefacts of a practice (philosophy) that *essentially projects an impossible achievement*. This impossibility is not the tantalizing incompleteness attendant on any asymptotic convergence (the young Husserl is said to have ground away the blade of his penknife trying to make it perfectly sharp), but a structural impossibility. For philosophy's goal has been a kind of semantic transparency, a subordination of linguistic means to authorial intentions, one that language both encourages and prevents. It encourages it by the illusion wrought by *living in* a language, of it having no determinate qualities. This is not a general prison-house of language thesis, but a specific one. For most practical purposes, inhabiting a natural language is what opens up the human world – not just literature and conversation, but science, business, law, politics and social life in general. If philosophy were just some higher grade practical enterprise then our difficulties would not arise. There are some voices, it is true, who have embraced this conclusion (Rorty, for example). But it is philosophy's quite peculiar power to take up such identifications, such verdicts on its own status, and problematize them.

The second supposition is that in the structure, style, strategy and even the project of philosophy there are possibilities of transformation, some of which have been explored, others glimpsed, and yet more only imagined. These possibilities, however, are not ways of scaling peaks that would yield to attempts using different equipment. It will no longer be true to say 'Because it was there' in answer to the question of why one made the attempt. The very landscape is new; philosophy has fallen down its rabbit-hole. But while there are clear parallels with Kant's transcendental method, we are no longer dealing with the hidden contribution of fundamental cognitive categories, or forms of intuition – not just, that is, with the *a priori* structure of 'knowledge' or 'experience'. What is at stake is the relation between the philosophical project itself and its textual mode of existence.

The first supposition is one of renunciation and caution in the light of an irresolvable complicity between thought and language. But does the philosophical project rest on a transcendence of this complicity? Or does this assessment reflect only a particular, perhaps dominant, metaphysical interpretation of that tradition? To suppose that it did would take us towards the second intuition. The recoil from philosophy's withdrawal from naive 'assertions about the world' fuels not only an interest in the whole range of possibilities of referential mediation, but also the other things that philosophy can do, and ways it can do them. At the same time, there is an interest in the structures constitutive of the philosophical project itself, as witness Gasché's development of Derrida's 'infrastructures' in *The Tain of the Mirror*. Such a development takes us towards the wider spaces of German idealism, which took philosophy beyond the problematics of representation in ways yet to be fully appreciated. Philosophy need not confine itself to policing the real by accounting for its possibility. It may yet again begin with the possible, and in the light of that interrogate the real. What is important this time round is to pursue this while at the same time deconstructing the discourse in which it is framed.

Some will see this as the grounds for an idealistic interpretation (and condemnation) of Derrida's famous claim that there is nothing beyond the text (see Chapter 3). But what is really at issue is the space in which the distinction between realism and idealism is being drawn. If it is one in which a naively representational model of the philosophical project is operating, then idealism will seem like some sort of error, failure or neglect. But once that project has been discredited, 'idealism' will have an entirely different significance, just as 'transcendental idealism' did for Kant. If some such move is accepted we find ourselves, as I have suggested, down the rabbit-hole (though not straightforwardly into nonsense).

I take sides with those arguments against the metaphysical goal of knowing the real or participation in it that treat this goal not simply as regrettably unachievable but as a delusion. This delusion can be understood as the supposition that the ordinary activities of reference to and description of the everyday world must have some higher theoretical analogues. But such a formulation explains nothing. A serious explanation might well pursue the structural invisibility of a language to its indwelling user, parallelling what Derrida describes in *Speech and Phenomena* as the ideal or phenomenological transparency of 'hearing oneself speak', in which one seems to be in direct contact with one's own meaning. I will not, however, venture such an explanation here. I have suggested two different ways of proceeding after the recoil from the project of penetrating the real. The first involves a transformation of how one writes philosophy, and the second involves a change in the domain of one's attentive exploration. To the extent that the domain in question is philosophy itself and its background assumptions, the second way is always already involved in the first. There can be no change of style or strategy or approach without some kind of grasp of how it would make a difference, which requires some thematic appreciation of philosophical textuality.

Can the second way, the exploration of new territory, be anything more than a handmaiden to the first, a change in one's mode, angle, orientation of philosophizing? The strongest argument against it having any distinct value is this: unless one insists on its contribution to a changing philosophical practice, it will give birth to another imaginary realm of discourse, like that of Husserl's sphere of transcendental subjectivity, a theatre for metaphysical activity. The temptation to such a move is enormous; it is as powerful as the original drive to some sort of coincidence with the real. It would even seem to allow renewed life to such a project, now productively displaced. But careful, analytical description of (say) quasi-transcendental structures still tacitly privileges description and leaves unthought, as Heidegger would put it, the being of 'description'. But in giving such a Heideggerian diagnosis of the problem, even by way of illustration, we confront an aporia of our own: for Heidegger's own attempt to give sense to such a diagnosis involved him in a further, deeper descriptive project – of fundamental ontology – a project that took for granted the very primacy of descriptive theorizing that is being put in question. The subsequent trajectory of Heidegger's thought reflects his own attempt to deal with this matter.

In this book, I have not addressed or pursued the problem at this level of reflexivity. I have supposed that I could write directly about the possibilities opened up by Kierkegaard's account (and practice) of indirect communication. I have argued for deconstruction to be accorded a privileged place in the pantheon of critical philosophical methods (even as it unsettles the very ideas of criticism and critique), without deploying deconstructive devices or strategies. I have traced through a deconstructive *argument* about the place of metaphor in philosophy, one that both affirms that place and questions the metaphysical credentials of 'metaphor' itself. I myself have engaged in neither purification nor systematic exploitation of metaphor. I have discussed in particular Nietzsche's own insistence on style, what I called a liminal textuality, without problematizing my own commitment to a kind of analytical clarity, albeit imperfectly realized. My discussion of the limits of *dialogue*, a value that seems fundamental to intellectual life, sought to disentangle the misunderstandings while highlighting the moves being made in the 'debate' between Derrida and Gadamer. My presentation of this debate involved no mimetic re-enactment, no refusal to explain, no gestures to radical otherness. I have not staged the kind of textual totalization, nor, in consequence engaged in the kind of self-dramatizing of philosophy as writing diagnosed in Hegel. Am I not obliged to explain the apparent contradiction? If I have been successful have I not demonstrated the possibility of a kind of domesticating analytical translation of all that is of lasting value in these continental thinkers?

The central philosophical aim of this book is to vindicate a certain species of *difficulty* in philosophy. Such difficulties proceed from paradoxes inherent in the most powerful formulations of the philosophical project and in the inherently *critical* dimension of philosophy, a dimension which affects its very own self-understanding. The transformation of the philosophical project is arguably a perennial task, and the curling back of critique onto itself is something philosophy can neither prevent, nor finally come to terms with. This essential restlessness is a necessary limit to a historically dominant conception of the philosophical project. Tracing the faces and forms of this limit in those works that stage it in exemplary ways *may* disturb the theatre of their performance; it is my hope that it will increase the demand for seats.

Index